Travel phrasebooks collection
«Everything Will Be Okay!»

T&P Books Publishing

PHRASEBOOK

— TAJIK —

I0163379

THE MOST IMPORTANT PHRASES

This phrasebook contains the most important phrases and questions for basic communication
Everything you need to survive overseas

By Andrey Taranov

T&P BOOKS

Phrasebook + 1500-word dictionary

English-Tajik phrasebook & concise dictionary

By Andrey Taranov

The collection of "Everything Will Be Okay" travel phrasebooks published by T&P Books is designed for people traveling abroad for tourism and business. The phrasebooks contain what matters most - the essentials for basic communication. This is an indispensable set of phrases to "survive" while abroad.

Another section of the book also provides a small dictionary with more than 1,500 useful words arranged alphabetically. The dictionary includes a lot of gastronomic terms and will be helpful when ordering food at a restaurant or buying groceries at the store.

T&P Books Publishing
www.tpbooks.com

ISBN: 978-1-78616-750-7

This book is also available in E-book formats.
Please visit www.tpbooks.com or the major online bookstores.

FOREWORD

The collection of "Everything Will Be Okay" travel phrasebooks published by T&P Books is designed for people traveling abroad for tourism and business. The phrasebooks contain what matters most - the essentials for basic communication. This is an indispensable set of phrases to "survive" while abroad.

This phrasebook will help you in most cases where you need to ask something, get directions, find out how much something costs, etc. It can also resolve difficult communication situations where gestures just won't help.

This book contains a lot of phrases that have been grouped according to the most relevant topics. A separate section of the book also provides a small dictionary with more than 1,500 important and useful words.

Take "Everything Will Be Okay" phrasebook with you on the road and you'll have an irreplaceable traveling companion who will help you find your way out of any situation and teach you to not fear speaking with foreigners.

TABLE OF CONTENTS

T&P Books Publishing

PRONUNCIATION

Letter	Tajik example	T&P phonetic alphabet	English example
А а	Раҳмат!	[a]	shorter than in ask
Б б	бесоҳиб	[b]	baby, book
В в	вафодорӣ	[v]	very, river
Г г	гулмоҳӣ	[g]	game, gold
Ғ ғ	мурғобӣ	[ʁ]	French (guttural) R
Д д	мадд	[d]	day, doctor
Е е	телескоп	[e:]	longer than in bell
Ё ё	сайёра	[jɔ]	New York
Ж ж	аждаҳо	[ʒ]	forge, pleasure
З з	сӯзанда	[z]	zebra, please
И и	шифт	[i]	shorter than in feet
Ӣ ӣ	обчакорӣ	[i:]	feet, meter
Й й	ҳайкал	[j]	yes, New York
К к	коргардон	[k]	clock, kiss
Қ қ	нуқта	[q]	king, club
Л л	пилла	[l]	lace, people
М м	мусиқачӣ	[m]	magic, milk
Н н	нонвой	[n]	sang, thing
О о	посбон	[o:]	fall, bomb
П п	папка	[p]	pencil, private
Р р	чароғак	[r]	rice, radio
С с	суръат	[s]	city, boss
Т т	тарқиш	[t]	tourist, trip
У у	муҳаррик	[u]	book
Ӯ ӯ	кӯшк	[œ]	German Hölle
Ф ф	фурӯш	[f]	face, food
Х х	хушксолӣ	[x]	as in Scots 'loch'
Ҳ ҳ	чарогоҳ	[h]	home, have
Ч ч	чароғ	[tʃ]	church, French
Ҷ ҷ	ҷанҷол	[ʤ]	joke, general
Ш ш	нашриёт	[ʃ]	machine, shark
Ъ ъ ¹	таърихдон	[:], [ʼ]	no sound
Э э	эҳтимолӣ	[ɛ]	man, bad
Ю ю	юнонӣ	[ju]	youth, usually
Я я	яхбурча	[ja]	Kenya, piano

Comments

[1] [:] - Lengthens the preceding vowel; ['] - after consonants is used as a 'hard sign'

LIST OF ABBREVIATIONS

English abbreviations

ab.	-	about
adj	-	adjective
adv	-	adverb
anim.	-	animate
as adj	-	attributive noun used as adjective
e.g.	-	for example
etc.	-	et cetera
fam.	-	familiar
fem.	-	feminine
form.	-	formal
inanim.	-	inanimate
masc.	-	masculine
math	-	mathematics
mil.	-	military
n	-	noun
pl	-	plural
pron.	-	pronoun
sb	-	somebody
sing.	-	singular
sth	-	something
v aux	-	auxiliary verb
vi	-	intransitive verb
vi, vt	-	intransitive, transitive verb
vt	-	transitive verb

TAJIK
PHRASEBOOK

This section contains
important phrases that may
come in handy in various
real-life situations.
The phrasebook will help
you ask for directions, clarify
a price, buy tickets, and
order food at a restaurant

T&P Books Publishing

PHRASEBOOK CONTENTS

T&P Books Publishing

The bare minimum

Excuse me, …	**Бубахшед, …** [bubaχʃed, …]
Hello.	**Салом.** [salom]
Thank you.	**Ташаккур.** [taʃakkur]
Good bye.	**То дидан.** [to didan]
Yes.	**Ҳа.** [ha]
No.	**Не.** [ne]
I don't know.	**Ман намедонам.** [man namedonam]
Where? | Where to? | When?	**Дар куҷо? | Ба куҷо? | Кай?** [dar kuʤo? | ba kuʤo? | kaj?]

I need …	**Ба ман … даркор аст.** [ba man … darkor ast]
I want …	**Ман … мехоҳам.** [man … meχoham]
Do you have …?	**Шумо … доред?** [ʃumo … dored?]
Is there a … here?	**Дар ин ҷо … ҳаст?** [dar in ʤo … hast?]
May I …?	**… метавонам?** [… metavonam?]
…, please (polite request)	**Илтимос** [iltimos]

I'm looking for …	**Ман … мекобам.** [man … mekobam]
restroom	**хоҷатхона** [χoʤatχona]
ATM	**худпардоз** [χudpardoz]
pharmacy (drugstore)	**дорухона** [doruχona]
hospital	**беморхона** [bemorχona]
police station	**идораи пулис** [idorai pulis]
subway	**метро** [metro]

taxi	**такси** [taksi]
train station	**вокзал** [vokzal]

My name is ...	**Номи ман ...** [nomi man ...]
What's your name?	**Номи шумо чӣ?** [nomi ʃumo tʃi:?]
Could you please help me?	**Илтимос, ба ман ёрӣ диҳед.** [iltimos, ba man jori: dihed]
I've got a problem.	**Ман мушкилӣ дорам.** [man muʃkili: doram]
I don't feel well.	**Худамро бад ҳис мекунам.** [χudamro bad his mekunam]
Call an ambulance!	**Ба ёрии таъҷилӣ занг занед!** [ba jorii ta'dʒili: zang zaned!]
May I make a call?	**Мумкин занг занам?** [mumkin zang zanam?]

I'm sorry.	**Бубахшед** [bubaχʃed]
You're welcome.	**Намеарзад** [namearzad]

I, me	**ман** [man]
you (inform.)	**ту** [tu]
he	**ӯ, вай** [œ, vaj]
she	**ӯ, вай** [œ, vaj]
they (masc.)	**онҳо** [onho]
they (fem.)	**онҳо** [onho]
we	**мо** [mo]
you (pl)	**шумо** [ʃumo]
you (sg, form.)	**Шумо** [ʃumo]

ENTRANCE	**ДАРОМАДГОҲ** [daromadgoh]
EXIT	**БАРОМАДГОҲ** [baromadgoh]
OUT OF ORDER	**КОР НАМЕКУНАД** [kor namekunad]
CLOSED	**ПӮШИДА** [pœʃida]

OPEN	**КУШОДА**
	[kuʃoda]
FOR WOMEN	**БАРОИ ЗАНОН**
	[baroi zanon]
FOR MEN	**БАРОИ МАРДОН**
	[baroi mardon]

Questions

Where?
Дар кучо?
[dar kudʒo?]

Where to?
Ба кучо?
[ba kudʒo?]

Where from?
Аз кучо?
[az kudʒo?]

Why?
Барои чӣ?
[baroi tʃi:?]

For what reason?
Чаро?
[tʃaro?]

When?
Кай?
[kaj?]

How long?
То кай?
[to kaj?]

At what time?
Дар соати чанд?
[dar soati tʃand?]

How much?
Чанд пул?
[tʃand pul?]

Do you have ...?
Шумо ... доред?
[ʃumo ... dored?]

Where is ...?
... дар кучо?
[... dar kudʒo?]

What time is it?
Соат чанд?
[soat tʃand?]

May I make a call?
Мумкин занг занам?
[mumkin zang zanam?]

Who's there?
Кӣ?
[ki:?]

Can I smoke here?
Дар ин чо сигор кашида метавонам?
[dar in dʒo sigor kaʃida metavonam?]

May I ...?
... метавонам?
[... metavonam?]

Needs

I'd like ...	**Ман ... мехостам.** [man ... meχostam]
I don't want ...	**... намехоҳам.** [... nameχoham]
I'm thirsty.	**Ман нӯшидан мехоҳам.** [man nœʃidan meχoham]
I want to sleep.	**Ман хоб дорам.** [man χob doram]

I want ...	**Ман ... мехоҳам.** [man ... meχoham]
to wash up	**шустушӯ кардан** [ʃustuʃœ kardan]
to brush my teeth	**дандон шустан** [dandon ʃustan]
to rest a while	**каме дам гирифтан** [kame dam giriftan]
to change my clothes	**либосамро иваз кардан** [libosamro ivaz kardan]

to go back to the hotel	**ба меҳмонхона баргаштан** [ba mehmonχona bargaʃtan]
to buy ...	**... харидан** [... χaridan]
to go to ...	**ба ... рафтан** [ba ... raftan]
to visit ...	**ба ... боздид кардан** [ba ... bozdid kardan]
to meet with ...	**вохӯрдан бо ...** [voχœrdan bo ...]
to make a call	**занг задан** [zang zadan]

I'm tired.	**Хаста шудам.** [χasta ʃudam]
We are tired.	**Хаста шудем.** [χasta ʃudem]
I'm cold.	**Хунук мехӯрам.** [χunuk meχœram]
I'm hot.	**Тафсидам.** [tafsidam]
I'm OK.	**Барои ман хуб.** [baroi man χub]

I need to make a call.

Ман бояд занг занам.
[man bojad zang zanam]

I need to go to the restroom.

Бояд ба ҳоҷатхона равам.
[bojad ba hoʤatχona ravam]

I have to go.

Бояд равам.
[bojad ravam]

I have to go now.

Ба ман рафтан лозим аст.
[ba man raftan lozim ast]

Asking for directions

Excuse me, …
Бубахшед, …
[bubaxʃed, …]

Where is …?
… дар кучо?
[… dar kuʤo?]

Which way is …?
… дар кадом самт аст?
[… dar kadom samt ast?]

Could you help me, please?
Илтимос, ба ман ёрй дихед.
[iltimos, ba man jori: dihed]

I'm looking for …
Ман … мекобам.
[man … mekobam]

I'm looking for the exit.
Ман баромадгох мекобам.
[man baromadgoh mekobam]

I'm going to …
Ман ба … меравам.
[man ba … meravam]

Am I going the right way to …?
Ман ба … дуруст меравам?
[man ba … durust meravam?]

Is it far?
Ин дур аст?
[in dur ast?]

Can I get there on foot?
Ба онҷо пиёда рафта метавонам?
[ba onʤo pijoda rafta metavonam?]

Can you show me on the map?
Илтимос, дар харита нишон диҳед.
[iltimos, dar xarita niʃon dihed]

Show me where we are right now.
Нишон диҳед, ки ҳоло мо дар кучо ҳастем.
[niʃon dihed, ki holo mo dar kuʤo hastem]

Here
Ин ҷо
[in ʤo]

There
Он ҷо
[on ʤo]

This way
Ба ин ҷо
[ba in ʤo]

Turn right.
Ба дасти рост гардед.
[ba dasti rost garded]

Turn left.
Ба дасти чап гардед.
[ba dasti tʃap garded]

first (second, third) turn
гардиши якум (дуюм, сеюм)
[gardiʃi jakum (dujum, sejum)]

to the right
Ба дасти рост
[ba dasti rost]

to the left	**Ба дасти чап** [ba dasti tʃap]
Go straight ahead.	**Рост равед.** [rost raved]

Signs

WELCOME!	**ХУШ ОМАДЕД!** [χuʃ omaded!]
ENTRANCE	**ДАРОМАДГОХ** [daromadgoh]
EXIT	**БАРОМАДГОХ** [baromadgoh]
PUSH	**АЗ ХУД** [az χud]
PULL	**БА ХУД** [ba χud]
OPEN	**КУШОДА** [kuʃoda]
CLOSED	**ПӮШИДА** [pœʃida]
FOR WOMEN	**БАРОИ ЗАНОН** [baroi zanon]
FOR MEN	**БАРОИ МАРДОН** [baroi mardon]
GENTLEMEN, GENTS (m)	**ХОҶАТХОНАИ МАРДОНА** [hoʤatχonai mardona]
WOMEN (f)	**ХОҶАТХОНАИ ЗАНОНА** [hoʤatχonai zanona]
DISCOUNTS	**ТАХФИФ** [taχfif]
SALE	**ҲАРОҶ** [haroʤ]
FREE	**РОЙГОН** [rojgon]
NEW!	**НАВБАРОМАД!** [navbaromad!]
ATTENTION!	**ДИҚҚАТ!** [diqqat!]
NO VACANCIES	**ҶОЙ НЕСТ** [ʤoj nest]
RESERVED	**БАНД АСТ** [band ast]
ADMINISTRATION	**МАЪМУРИЯТ** [ma'murijat]
STAFF ONLY	**ТАНҲО БАРОИ ҲАЙАТ** [tanho baroi hajat]

BEWARE OF THE DOG! **САГИ ГАЗАНДА**
[sagi gazanda]

NO SMOKING! **СИГОР НАКАШЕД!**
[sigor nakaʃed!]

DO NOT TOUCH! **ЛАМС НАКУНЕД!**
[lams nakuned!]

DANGEROUS **ХАТАРНОК**
[xatarnok]

DANGER **ХАТАР**
[xatar]

HIGH VOLTAGE **ШИДДАТИ БАЛАНД**
[ʃiddati baland]

NO SWIMMING! **ОББОЗӢ МАНЪ АСТ**
[obbozi: man' ast]

OUT OF ORDER **КОР НАМЕКУНАД**
[kor namekunad]

FLAMMABLE **ОТАШАНГЕЗ**
[otaʃangez]

FORBIDDEN **МАНЪ АСТ**
[man' ast]

NO TRESPASSING! **ГУЗАШТАН МАНЪ АСТ**
[guzaʃtan man' ast]

WET PAINT **РАНГ КАРДА ШУДААСТ**
[rang karda ʃudaast]

CLOSED FOR RENOVATIONS **ПӮШИДА, ТАЪМИР МЕРАВАД**
[pœʃida, ta'mir meravad]

WORKS AHEAD **ТАЪМИРИ РОҲ**
[ta'miri roh]

DETOUR **РОҲИ ДАВРОДАВР**
[rohi davrodavr]

Transportation. General phrases

plane	**тайёра** [tajjora]
train	**қатор** [qator]
bus	**автобус** [avtobus]
ferry	**паром** [parom]
taxi	**такси** [taksi]
car	**мошин** [moʃin]

schedule	**ҷадвал** [dʒadval]
Where can I see the schedule?	**Ҷадвалро дар куҷо дидан мумкин?** [dʒadvalro dar kudʒo didan mumkin?]
workdays (weekdays)	**рӯзҳои корӣ** [rœzhoi kori:]
weekends	**рӯзҳои истироҳат** [rœzhoi istirohat]
holidays	**рӯзҳои идона** [rœzhoi idona]

DEPARTURE	**ХУРУҶ** [xurudʒ]
ARRIVAL	**ВУРУД** [vurud]
DELAYED	**ТАЪХИР ДОРАД** [ta'xir dorad]
CANCELLED	**ЛАҒВ ШУД** [laǧv ʃud]

next (train, etc.)	**навбатӣ** [navbati:]
first	**якум** [jakum]
last	**охирон** [oxiron]

When is the next …?	**… навбатӣ кай меояд?** [… navbati: kaj meojad?]
When is the first …?	**… якум кай меравад?** [… jakum kaj meravad?]

When is the last …?

… охирон кай меравад?
[… oχiron kaj meravad?]

transfer (change of trains, etc.)

гузариш
[guzariʃ]

to make a transfer

буро-фуро кардан
[buro-furo kardan]

Do I need to make a transfer?

Ба ман буро-фуро кардан лозим.
[ba man buro-furo kardan lozim]

Buying tickets

Where can I buy tickets?	**Чиптаҳоро аз куҷо харида метавонам?** [tʃiptahoro az kudʒo χarida metavonam?]
ticket	**чипта** [tʃipta]
to buy a ticket	**чипта харидан** [tʃipta χaridan]
ticket price	**нархи чипта** [narχi tʃipta]

Where to?	**Ба куҷо?** [ba kudʒo?]
To what station?	**То кадом истгоҳ?** [to kadom istgoh?]
I need ...	**Ба ман ... даркор аст.** [ba man ... darkor ast]
one ticket	**як чипта** [jak tʃipta]
two tickets	**ду чипта** [du tʃipta]
three tickets	**се чипта** [se tʃipta]
one-way	**ба як тараф** [ba jak taraf]
round-trip	**ба ҳар ду тараф** [ba har du taraf]
first class	**дараҷаи якум** [daradʒai jakum]
second class	**дараҷаи дуюм** [daradʒai dujum]

today	**имрӯз** [imrœz]
tomorrow	**фардо** [fardo]
the day after tomorrow	**пасфардо** [pasfardo]
in the morning	**саҳарӣ** [sahari:]
in the afternoon	**рӯзона** [rœzona]
in the evening	**бегоҳӣ** [begohi:]

aisle seat

ҷойи назди гузаргоҳ
[dʒoji nazdi guzargoh]

window seat

ҷойи назди тиреза
[dʒoji nazdi tireza]

How much?

Чанд-то?
[tʃand-to?]

Can I pay by credit card?

Бо корт пардохтан мумкин?
[bo kort pardoxtan mumkin?]

Bus

bus	**автобус** [avtobus]
intercity bus	**автобуси байнишаҳрӣ** [avtobusi bajniʃahri:]
bus stop	**истогоҳи автобус** [istogohi avtobus]
Where's the nearest bus stop?	**Наздиктарин истогоҳи автобус дар куҷо?** [nazdiktarin istogohi avtobus dar kuʤo?]

number (bus ~, etc.)	**рақам** [raqam]
Which bus do I take to get to …?	**Кадом автобус ба … мебарад?** [kadom avtobus ba … mebarad?]
Does this bus go to …?	**Ин автобус то … мебарад?** [in avtobus to … mebarad?]
How frequent are the buses?	**Автобусҳо зуд-зуд мегарданд?** [avtobusho zud-zud megardand?]

every 15 minutes	**ҳар понздаҳ дақиқа** [har ponzdah daqiqa]
every half hour	**ҳар ним соат** [har nim soat]
every hour	**ҳар соат** [har soat]

several times a day	**якчанд маротиба дар рӯз** [jaktʃand marotiba dar rœz]
… times a day	**… бор дар як рӯз.** [… bor dar jak rœz]

schedule	**ҷадвал** [ʤadval]
Where can I see the schedule?	**Ҷадвалро дар куҷо дидан мумкин?** [ʤadvalro dar kuʤo didan mumkin?]

When is the next bus?	**автобуси навбатӣ кай меояд?** [avtobusi navbati: kaj meojad?]
When is the first bus?	**автобуси якум кай меравад?** [avtobusi jakum kaj meravad?]
When is the last bus?	**автобуси охирон кай меравад?** [avtobusi oҳiron kaj meravad?]

stop

истгоҳ
[istgoh]

next stop

истгоҳи оянда
[istgohi ojanda]

last stop (terminus)

истгоҳи охир
[istgohi oχir]

Stop here, please.

Лутфан, дар ҳамин ҷо нигоҳ доред.
[lutfan, dar hamin ʤo nigoh dored]

Excuse me, this is my stop.

Иҷозат диҳед, ин истгоҳи ман аст.
[idʒozat dihed, in istgohi man ast]

Train

train	**қатор** [qator]
suburban train	**қатори наздишаҳрӣ** [qatori nazdiʃahri:]
long-distance train	**қатори дуррав** [qatori durrav]
train station	**вокзал** [vokzal]
Excuse me, where is the exit to the platform?	**Бубахшед, баромадгоҳ ба назди қаторҳо дар куҷо?** [bubaxʃed, baromadgoh ba nazdi qatorho dar kuʤo?]

Does this train go to ...?	**Ин қатор то ... мебарад?** [in qator to ... mebarad?]
next train	**қатори навбатӣ** [qatori navbati:]
When is the next train?	**Қатори навбатӣ кай меояд?** [qatori navbati: kaj meojad?]
Where can I see the schedule?	**Ҷадвалро дар куҷо дидан мумкин?** [ʤadvalro dar kuʤo didan mumkin?]
From which platform?	**Аз кадом платформа?** [az kadom platforma?]
When does the train arrive in ...?	**Қатор ба ... кай мерасад?** [qator ba ... kaj merasad?]

Please help me.	**Илтимос, ба ман ёрӣ диҳед.** [iltimos, ba man jori: dihed]
I'm looking for my seat.	**Ман ҷоямро мекобам.** [man ʤojamro mekobam]
We're looking for our seats.	**Мо ҷойҳоямонро меҷӯем.** [mo ʤojhojamonro meʤœem]
My seat is taken.	**Ҷойи ман банд аст.** [ʤoji man band ast]
Our seats are taken.	**Ҷойҳои мо бонданд.** [ʤojhoi mo bandand]

I'm sorry but this is my seat.	**Бубахшед, лекин ин ҷойи ман аст.** [bubaxʃed, lekin in ʤoji man ast.]
Is this seat taken?	**Ин ҷой озод аст?** [in ʤoj ozod ast?]
May I sit here?	**Ба ин ҷо шиштан мумкин?** [ba in ʤo ʃiʃtan mumkin?]

On the train. Dialogue (No ticket)

Ticket, please.

Лутфан, чиптаи шумо.
[lutfan, tʃiptai ʃumo]

I don't have a ticket.

Ман чипта надорам.
[man tʃipta nadoram]

I lost my ticket.

Ман чиптаамро гум кардам.
[man tʃiptaamro gum kardam]

I forgot my ticket at home.

Ман чиптаамро дар хона мондам.
[man tʃiptaamro dar χona mondam]

You can buy a ticket from me.

Шумо аз ман чипта харида метавонед.
[ʃumo az man tʃipta χarida metavoned]

You will also have to pay a fine.

Боз шумо бояд ҷарима супоред.
[boz ʃumo bojad dʒarima supored]

Okay.

Хуб.
[χub]

Where are you going?

Шумо ба куҷо сафар доред?
[ʃumo ba kudʒo safar dored?]

I'm going to …

Ман то ... меравам.
[man to ... meravam]

How much? I don't understand.

Чанд? Ман намефаҳмам.
[tʃand? man namefahmam]

Write it down, please.

Илтимос, нависед.
[iltimos, navised]

Okay. Can I pay with a credit card?

Хуб. Бо корт пардохт карда метавонам?
[χub. bo kort pardoχt karda metavonam?]

Yes, you can.

Бале, метавонед.
[bale, metavoned]

Here's your receipt.

Ана квитансияи шумо.
[ana kvitansijai ʃumo]

Sorry about the fine.

Барои ҷарима афсӯс мехӯрам.
[baroi dʒarima afsœs meχœram]

That's okay. It was my fault.

Ҳеҷ гап не. Айби худам.
[hedʒ gap ne. ajbi χudam]

Enjoy your trip.

Роҳи сафед.
[rohi safed]

Taxi

taxi	**такси** [taksi]
taxi driver	**ронандаи такси, таксичӣ** [ronandai taksi, taksitʃi:]
to catch a taxi	**такси гирифтан** [taksi giriftan]
taxi stand	**истгоҳи такси** [istgohi taksi]
Where can I get a taxi?	**Дар куҷо такси ёфта метавонам?** [dar kudʒo taksi jofta metavonam?]
to call a taxi	**такси фармудан** [taksi farmudan]
I need a taxi.	**Ба ман такси даркор аст.** [ba man taksi darkor ast]
Right now.	**Худи ҳозир.** [χudi hozir]
What is your address (location)?	**Нишонии шумо?** [niʃonii ʃumo?]
My address is …	**Нишонии ман …** [niʃonii man …]
Your destination?	**Ба куҷо меравед?** [ba kudʒo meraved?]
Excuse me, …	**Бубахшед, …** [bubaχʃed, …]
Are you available?	**Шумо озод?** [ʃumo ozod?]
How much is it to get to …?	**То ба … чанд пул мешавад?** [to ba … tʃand pul meʃavad?]
Do you know where it is?	**Шумо дар куҷо буданашро медонед?** [ʃumo dar kudʒo budanaʃro medoned?]
Airport, please.	**Ба фурудгоҳ, хоҳиш мекунам.** [ba furudgoh, χohiʃ mekunam]
Stop here, please.	**Лутфан, дар ҳамин ҷо нигоҳ доред.** [lutfan, dar hamin dʒo nigoh dored]
It's not here.	**Дар ин ҷо не.** [dar in dʒo ne]
This is the wrong address.	**Ин нишонии ғалат аст.** [in niʃonii ğalat ast]

Turn left.

Ҳоло ба чап.
[holo ba tʃap]

Turn right.

Ҳоло ба рост.
[holo ba rost]

How much do I owe you?

Чанд пул бояд диҳам?
[tʃand pul bojad diham?]

I'd like a receipt, please.

Лутфан, ба ман чек диҳед.
[lutfan, ba man tʃek dihed]

Keep the change.

Бақия лозим нест.
[baqija lozim nest]

Would you please wait for me?

Лутфан, маро мунтазир шавед.
[lutfan, maro muntazir ʃaved]

five minutes

панҷ дақиқа
[pandʒ daqiqa]

ten minutes

даҳ дақиқа
[dah daqiqa]

fifteen minutes

понздаҳ дақиқа
[ponzdah daqiqa]

twenty minutes

бист дақиқа
[bist daqiqa]

half an hour

ним соат
[nim soat]

Hotel

Hello.	**Салом.** [salom]
My name is …	**Номи ман …** [nomi man …]
I have a reservation.	**Утоқеро резерв кардам.** [utoqero rezerv kardam]
I need …	**Ба ман … даркор аст.** [ba man … darkor ast]
a single room	**утоқи якнафара** [utoqi jaknafara]
a double room	**утоқи дунафара** [utoqi dunafara]
How much is that?	**Он чанд пул аст?** [on tʃand pul ast?]
That's a bit expensive.	**Ин каме қимат аст.** [in kame qimat ast]
Do you have anything else?	**Шумо боз ягон чизи дигар доред?** [ʃumo boz jagon tʃizi digar dored?]
I'll take it.	**Ман онро мегирам.** [man onro megiram]
I'll pay in cash.	**Ман пули нақд медиҳам.** [man puli naqd mediham]
I've got a problem.	**Ман мушкилӣ дорам.** [man muʃkili: doram]
My … is broken.	**… ман шикастагӣ.** [… man ʃikastagi:]
My … is out of order.	**… ман кор намекунад.** [… man kor namekunad]
TV	**телевизор** [televizor]
air conditioner	**кондитсионер** [konditsioner]
tap	**кран** [kran]
shower	**душ** [duʃ]
sink	**дастшӯяк** [dastʃœjak]
safe	**сейф** [sejf]

door lock	**қуфл** [qufl]
electrical outlet	**розетка** [rozetka]
hairdryer	**фен** [fen]

I don't have …	**Ман ... надорам.** [man ... nadoram]
water	**об** [ob]
light	**нури чароғ** [nuri tʃaroğ]
electricity	**барқ** [barq]

Can you give me …?	**Ба ман ... дода метавонед?** [ba man ... doda metavoned?]
a towel	**дастрӯймол** [dastrœjmol]
a blanket	**кӯрпа** [kœrpa]
slippers	**шиппак** [ʃippak]
a robe	**халат** [χalat]
shampoo	**шампун** [ʃampun]
soap	**собун** [sobun]

I'd like to change rooms.	**Утоқамро иваз кардан мехостам.** [utoqamro ivaz kardan meχostam]
I can't find my key.	**Ман калидамро ёфта наметавонам.** [man kalidamro jofta nametavonam]
Could you open my room, please?	**Илтимос, утоқи маро кушоед.** [iltimos, utoqi maro kuʃoed]
Who's there?	**Кӣ?** [ki:?]
Come in!	**Дароед!** [daroed!]
Just a minute!	**Як дақиқа!** [jak daqiqa!]
Not right now, please.	**Илтимос, ҳозир не.** [iltimos, hozir ne]

Come to my room, please.	**Марҳамат, ба утоқи ман дароед.** [marhamat, ba utoqi man daroed]
I'd like to order food service.	**Мехоҳам бифармоям, ки хӯрокро ба утоқам биёранд.** [meχoham bifarmojam, ki χœrokro ba utoqam bijorand]

My room number is …

Рақами утоқи ман …
[raqami utoqi man …]

I'm leaving …

… ман аз ин ҷо меравам.
[… man az in dʒo meravam]

We're leaving …

… мо аз ин ҷо меравем.
[… mo az in dʒo meravem]

right now

ҳозир
[hozir]

this afternoon

имрӯз, пас аз хӯроки нисфирӯзй
[imrœz, pas az xœroki nisfirœzi:]

tonight

имрӯз бегоҳй
[imrœz begohi:]

tomorrow

фардо
[fardo]

tomorrow morning

субҳи фардо
[subhi fardo]

tomorrow evening

шоми фардо
[ʃomi fardo]

the day after tomorrow

пасфардо
[pasfardo]

I'd like to pay.

Аз ман чанд пул?
[az man tʃand pul?]

Everything was wonderful.

Ҳамааш олй буд.
[hamaaʃ oli: bud]

Where can I get a taxi?

Дар куҷо такси ёфта метавонам?
[dar kudʒo taksi jofta metavonam?]

Would you call a taxi for me, please?

Илтимос, ба ман такси фармоед.
[iltimos, ba man taksi farmoed]

Restaurant

Can I look at the menu, please?
Менюи шуморо дидан мумкин?
[menjui ʃumoro didan mumkin?]

Table for one.
Миз барои як кас.
[miz baroi jak kas]

There are two (three, four) of us.
Мо ду (се, чор) кас.
[mo du (se, tʃor) kas]

Smoking
Барои сигор мекашидагихо
[baroi sigor mekaʃidagiho]

No smoking
Барои сигор намекашидагихо
[baroi sigor namekaʃidagiho]

Excuse me! (addressing a waiter)
Лутфан!
[lutfan!]

menu
меню, номгӯйи хӯрокхо
[menju, nomgœji xœrokho]

wine list
корти майхо
[korti majho]

The menu, please.
Меню, лутфан.
[menju, lutfan]

Are you ready to order?
Шумо ба фармоиш додан омода ҳастед?
[ʃumo ba farmoiʃ dodan omoda hasted?]

What will you have?
Чй мефармоед?
[tʃi: mefarmoed?]

I'll have ...
Ба ман ... биёред.
[ba man ... bijored]

I'm a vegetarian.
Ман гиёҳхӯр ҳастам.
[man gijohxœr hastam]

meat
гӯшт
[gœʃt]

fish
моҳй
[mohi:]

vegetables
сабзавот
[sabzavot]

Do you have vegetarian dishes?
Шумо хӯрокхои бегӯшт доред?
[ʃumo xœrokhoi begœʃt dored?]

I don't eat pork.
Ман гӯшти хук намехӯрам.
[man gœʃti xuk namexœram]

He /she/ doesn't eat meat.
Ӯ гӯшт намехӯрад.
[œ gœʃt namexœrad]

I am allergic to ...

Ман ба ... ҳассосият дорам.
[man ba ... hassosijat doram]

Would you please bring me ...

Лутфан, ба ман ... биёред.
[lutfan, ba man ... bijored]

salt | pepper | sugar

намак | мурч | шакар
[namak | murtʃ | ʃakar]

coffee | tea | dessert

қаҳва | чой | ширинӣ
[qahva | tʃoj | ʃirini:]

water | sparkling | plain

об | газнок | бе газ
[ob | gaznok | be gaz]

a spoon | fork | knife

қошуқ | чангол | корд
[qoʃuq | tʃangol | kord]

a plate | napkin

табақча | дастмол
[tabaqtʃa | dastmol]

Enjoy your meal!

Иштиҳои том!
[iʃtihoi tom!]

One more, please.

Лутфан, боз биёред.
[lutfan, boz bijored]

It was very delicious.

Хеле бомаза буд.
[χele bomaza bud]

---

check | change | tip

ҳисобӣ | бақия | чойпулӣ
[ɦisobi: | baqija | tʃojpuli:]

Check, please.
(Could I have the check, please?)

Лутфан, ҳисоб кунед.
[lutfan, hisob kuned]

Can I pay by credit card?

Бо корт пардохта метавонам?
[bo kort pardoχta metavonam?]

I'm sorry, there's a mistake here.

Бубахшед, дар ин ҷо хато шудааст.
[bubaχʃed, dar in dʒo χato ʃudaast]

Shopping

Can I help you?
Метавонам ба шумо ёрй диҳам?
[metavonam ba ʃumo jori: diham?]

Do you have …?
Шумо … доред?
[ʃumo … dored?]

I'm looking for …
Ман … мекобам.
[man … mekobam]

I need …
Ба ман … даркор аст.
[ba man … darkor ast]

I'm just looking.
Ҳамту тамошо мекунам.
[hamtu tamoʃo mekunam]

We're just looking.
Мо ҳамту тамошо мекунем
[mo hamtu tamoʃo mekunem]

I'll come back later.
Ман дертар меоям.
[man dertar meojam]

We'll come back later.
Мо дертар меоем.
[mo dertar meoem]

discounts | sale
таҳфиф | ҳароҷ
[tahfif | harodʒ]

Would you please show me …
Лутфан, ба ман … нишон диҳед.
[lutfan, ba man … niʃon dihed]

Would you please give me …
Лутфан, ба ман … диҳед.
[lutfan, ba man … dihed]

Can I try it on?
Мумкин инро пӯшида бинам?
[mumkin inro pœʃida binam?]

Excuse me, where's the fitting room?
Ҷойи пӯшида дидан дар куҷо?
[dʒoji pœʃida didan dar kudʒo?]

Which color would you like?
Кадом рангашро мехоҳед?
[kadom rangaʃro meχohed?]

size | length
андоза | қад
[andoza | qad]

How does it fit?
Чен аст?
[tʃen ast?]

How much is it?
Ин чанд пул?
[in tʃand pul?]

That's too expensive.
Ин хеле қимат.
[in χele qimat]

I'll take it.
Ман инро мегирам.
[man inro megiram]

Excuse me, where do I pay?
Бубахшед, касса дар куҷо?
[bubaχʃed, kassa dar kudʒo?]

Will you pay in cash or credit card?

Чӣ гуна пардохт мекунед?
Бо пули нақд ё бо корт?
[tʃi: guna pardoχt mekuned?
bo puli naqd jo bo kort?]

In cash | with credit card

нақд | бо корт
[naqd | bo kort]

Do you want the receipt?

Ба шумо чек лозим?
[ba ʃumo tʃek lozim?]

Yes, please.

Бале, хоҳиш мекунам.
[bale, χohiʃ mekunam]

No, it's OK.

Не, лозим нест. Ташаккур.
[ne, lozim nest. taʃakkur]

Thank you. Have a nice day!

Ташаккур. Хуш бошед!
[taʃakkur. χuʃ boʃed!]

In town

Excuse me, please.	**Бубахшед, ...** [bubaχʃed, ...]
I'm looking for ...	**Ман ... мекобам.** [man ... mekobam]
the subway	**метро** [metro]
my hotel	**меҳмонхонаамро** [mehmonχonaamro]
the movie theater	**синамо** [sinamo]
a taxi stand	**истгоҳи таскӣ** [istgohi taski]

an ATM	**худпардоз** [χudpardoz]
a foreign exchange office	**мубодилаи асъор** [mubodilai as'or]
an internet café	**интернет-қаҳвахона** [internet-qahvaχona]
... street	**кӯчаи ...** [kœtʃai ...]
this place	**ана ин ҷо** [ana in dʒo]

Do you know where ... is?	**Шумо медонед, ки ... дар куҷо аст?** [ʃumo medoned, ki ... dar kudʒo ast?]
Which street is this?	**Ин кӯча чӣ ном дорад?** [in kœtʃa tʃi: nom dorad?]
Show me where we are right now.	**Нишон диҳед, ки холо мо дар куҷо ҳастем.** [niʃon dihed, ki holo mo dar kudʒo hastem]
Can I get there on foot?	**Ба онҷо пиёда рафта метавонам?** [ba ondʒo pijoda rafta metavonam?]
Do you have a map of the city?	**Шумо харитаи шаҳрро доред?** [ʃumo χaritai ʃahrro dored?]

How much is a ticket to get in?	**Чиптаи даромад чанд пул?** [tʃiptai daromad tʃand pul?]
Can I take pictures here?	**Дар ин ҷо сурат гирифтан мумкин?** [dar in dʒo surat giriftan mumkin?]
Are you open?	**Шумо кушода?** [ʃumo kuʃoda?]

When do you open?

Соати чанд кушода мешавед?
[soati tʃand kuʃoda meʃaved?]

When do you close?

То соати чанд кор мекунед?
[to soati tʃand kor mekuned?]

Money

money	**пул** [pul]
cash	**пули нақд** [puli naqd]
paper money	**пули қоғазӣ** [puli qoğazi:]
loose change	**пули майда** [puli majda]
check | change | tip	**ҳисобӣ | бақия | чойпулӣ** [hisobi: | baqija | tʃojpuli:]

credit card	**корти пластикӣ** [korti plastiki:]
wallet	**ҳамён** [hamjon]
to buy	**харид кардан** [χarid kardan]
to pay	**пардохтан** [pardoχtan]
fine	**ҷарима** [dʒarima]
free	**ройгон, бепул** [rojgon, bepul]

Where can I buy …?	**… аз куҷо харида метавонам?** [… az kudʒo χarida metavonam?]
Is the bank open now?	**Ҳоло бонк кушода аст?** [holo bonk kuʃoda ast?]
When does it open?	**Соати чанд кушода мешавад?** [soati tʃand kuʃoda meʃavad?]
When does it close?	**То соати чанд кор мекунад?** [to soati tʃand kor mekunad?]

How much?	**Чанд?** [tʃand?]
How much is this?	**Ин чанд пул?** [in tʃand pul?]
That's too expensive.	**Ин хеле қимат.** [in χele qimat]

Excuse me, where do I pay?	**Бубахшед, касса дар куҷо?** [bubaχʃed, kassa dar kudʒo?]
Check, please.	**Лутфан, ҳисоби моро биёред.** [lutfan, hisobi moro bijored]

Can I pay by credit card?

Бо корт пардохт кардан мумкин?
[bo kort pardoχt kardan mumkin?]

Is there an ATM here?

Дар ин ҷо худпардоз ҳаст?
[dar in dʒo χudpardoz hast?]

I'm looking for an ATM.

Ба ман худпардоз лозим аст.
[ba man χudpardoz lozim ast]

I'm looking for a foreign exchange office.

Ман саррофӣ мекобам.
[man sarrofi: mekobam]

I'd like to change …

… иваз кардан мехостам.
[… ivaz kardan meχostam]

What is the exchange rate?

Нархи арз чи қадр аст?
[narχi arz tʃi qadr ast?]

Do you need my passport?

Ба шумо шиносномаи ман даркор?
[ba ʃumo ʃinosnomai man darkor?]

Time

What time is it?	**Соат чанд?** [soat tʃand?]
When?	**Кай?** [kaj?]
At what time?	**Соати чанд?** [soati tʃand?]
now | later | after …	**ҳозир | дертар | баъди …** [hozir | dertar | ba'di …]
one o'clock	**яки рӯз** [jaki rœz]
one fifteen	**яку понздаҳ** [jaku ponzdah]
one thirty	**яку ним** [jaku nim]
one forty-five	**понздаҳто кам ду** [ponzdahto kam du]

one | two | three	**як | ду | се** [jak | du | se]
four | five | six	**чор | панҷ | шаш** [tʃor | pandʒ | ʃaʃ]
seven | eight | nine	**ҳафт | ҳашт | нӯҳ** [haft | haʃt | nœh]
ten | eleven | twelve	**даҳ | ёздаҳ | дувоздаҳ** [dah | jozdah | duvozdah]

in …	**баъди …** [ba'di …]
five minutes	**панҷ дақиқа** [pandʒ daqiqa]
ten minutes	**даҳ дақиқа** [dah daqiqa]
fifteen minutes	**понздаҳ дақиқа** [ponzdah daqiqa]
twenty minutes	**бист дақиқа** [bist daqiqa]
half an hour	**ним соат** [nim soat]
an hour	**як соат** [jak soat]
in the morning	**саҳарӣ** [sahari:]
early in the morning	**саҳари барвақт** [sahari barvaqt]

this morning	имрӯз саҳарӣ
	[imrœz sahari:]
tomorrow morning	субҳи фардо
	[subhi fardo]

in the middle of the day	дар нисфирӯзӣ
	[dar nisfirœzi:]
in the afternoon	баъди нисфирӯзӣ
	[ba'di nisfirœzi:]
in the evening	бегоҳӣ
	[begohi:]
tonight	имрӯз бегоҳӣ
	[imrœz begohi:]

at night	шабона
	[ʃabona]
yesterday	дирӯз
	[dirœz]
today	имрӯз
	[imrœz]
tomorrow	пагоҳ
	[pagoh]
the day after tomorrow	пасфардо
	[pasfardo]

What day is it today?	Имрӯз кадом рӯз аст?
	[imrœz kadom rœz ast?]
It's ...	Имрӯз ...
	[imrœz ...]
Monday	душанбе
	[duʃanbe]
Tuesday	сешанбе
	[seʃanbe]
Wednesday	чоршанбе
	[tʃorʃanbe]

Thursday	панҷшанбе
	[pandʒʃanbe]
Friday	ҷумъа
	[dʒum'a]
Saturday	шанбе
	[ʃanbe]
Sunday	якшанбе
	[jakʃanbe]

Greetings. Introductions

Hello.
Салом.
[salom]

Pleased to meet you.
Аз шиносой бо шумо хурсандам.
[az ʃinosoi: bo ʃumo χursandam]

Me too.
Ман ҳам.
[man ham]

I'd like you to meet …
Шинос шавед. Ин кас …
[ʃinos ʃaved. in kas …]

Nice to meet you.
Аз ошной бо шумо шод шудам.
[az oʃnoi: bo ʃumo ʃod ʃudam]

How are you?
Шумо чй хел? Корҳоятон чй хел?
[ʃumo tʃi: χel? korhojaton tʃi: χel?]

My name is …
Номи ман …
[nomi man …]

His name is …
Номи вай …
[nomi vaj …]

Her name is …
Номи вай …
[nomi vaj …]

What's your name?
Номи шумо чй?
[nomi ʃumo tʃi:?]

What's his name?
Номи вай чй?
[nomi vaj tʃi:?]

What's her name?
Номи вай чй?
[nomi vaj tʃi:?]

What's your last name?
Насаби шумо чй?
[nasabi ʃumo tʃi:?]

You can call me …
Маро … ном гиред.
[maro … nom gired]

Where are you from?
Шумо аз куҷо?
[ʃumo az kudʒo?]

I'm from …
Ман аз …
[man az …]

What do you do for a living?
Кй шуда кор мекунед?
[ki: ʃuda kor mekuned?]

Who is this?
Ин кй?
[in ki:?]

Who is he?
Вай кй?
[vaj ki:?]

Who is she?
Вай кй?
[vaj ki:?]

Who are they?	Онҳо кӣ?
	[onho ki:?]
This is ...	Ин кас ...
	[in kas ...]
my friend (masc.)	дӯсти ман
	[dœsti man]
my friend (fem.)	дугонаи ман
	[dugonai man]
my husband	шавҳари ман
	[ʃavhari man]
my wife	завҷаи ман
	[zavdʒai man]

my father	падари ман
	[padari man]
my mother	модари ман
	[modari man]
my brother	бародари ман
	[barodari man]
my sister	хоҳари ман
	[χohari man]
my son	писари ман
	[pisari man]
my daughter	духтари ман
	[duχtari man]

This is our son.	Ин писари мо.
	[in pisari mo]
This is our daughter.	Ин духтари мо.
	[in duχtari mo]
These are my children.	Инҳо фарзандони ман.
	[inho farzandoni man]
These are our children.	Инҳо фарзандони мо.
	[inho farzandoni mo]

Farewells

Good bye!
То дидан!
[to didan!]

Bye! (inform.)
Хайр!
[χajr!]

See you tomorrow.
То пагоҳ.
[to pagoh]

See you soon.
То боздид.
[to bozdid]

See you at seven.
Соати ҳафт вомехӯрем.
[soati haft vomeχœrem]

Have fun!
Вақтхушӣ кунед!
[vaqtχuʃi: kuned!]

Talk to you later.
Дертар гап мезанем.
[dertar gap mezanem]

Have a nice weekend.
Рӯзҳои истироҳатро хуб гузаронед.
[rœzhoi istirohatro χub guzaroned]

Good night.
Шаби хуш.
[ʃabi χuʃ]

It's time for me to go.
Бояд равам.
[bojad ravam]

I have to go.
Бояд равам.
[bojad ravam]

I will be right back.
Ман ҳозир бармегардам.
[man hozir barmegardam]

It's late.
Хеле бевақт шуд.
[χele bevaqt ʃud]

I have to get up early.
Пагоҳ бояд барвақт хезам.
[pagoh bojad barvaqt χezam]

I'm leaving tomorrow.
Пагоҳ ман меравам.
[pagoh man meravam]

We're leaving tomorrow.
Пагоҳ мо меравем.
[pagoh mo meravem]

Have a nice trip!
Роҳи сафед!
[rohi safed!]

It was nice meeting you.
Хурсандам, ки бо шумо шинос шудам.
[χursandam, ki bo ʃumo ʃinos ʃudam]

It was nice talking to you.
Аз суҳбати шумо баҳра бурдам.
[az suhbati ʃumo bahra burdam]

Thanks for everything.

Ташаккур барои ҳама чиз.
[taʃakkur baroi hama tʃiz]

I had a very good time.

Вақтам хеле хуб гузашт.
[vaqtam χele χub guzaʃt]

We had a very good time.

Вақтамон хеле хуб гузашт.
[vaqtamon χele χub guzaʃt]

It was really great.

Ҳама чиз олӣ буд.
[hama tʃiz oli: bud]

I'm going to miss you.

Ёд мекунам.
[jod mekunam]

We're going to miss you.

Мо ёд мекунем.
[mo jod mekunem]

Good luck!

Комрон бош! Хайр!
[komron boʃ! χajr!]

Say hi to …

Ба ... салом расонед.
[ba ... salom rasoned]

Foreign language

I don't understand.	**Ман намефаҳмам.** [man namefahmam]
Write it down, please.	**Лутфан, инро бинависед.** [lutfan, inro binavised]
Do you speak ...?	**Шумо забони ... медонед?** [ʃumo zaboni ... medoned?]

I speak a little bit of ...	**Каме ... медонам** [kame ... medonam]
English	**инглисӣ** [inglisi:]
Turkish	**туркӣ** [turki:]
Arabic	**арабӣ** [arabi:]
French	**фаронсавӣ** [faronsavi:]

German	**олмонӣ** [olmoni:]
Italian	**итолиёӣ** [itolijoi:]
Spanish	**испанӣ** [ispani:]
Portuguese	**португалӣ** [portugali:]
Chinese	**чинӣ** [tʃini:]
Japanese	**ҷопонӣ** [dʒoponi:]

Can you repeat that, please.	**Лутфан, такрор кунед.** [lutfan, takror kuned]
I understand.	**Мефаҳмам.** [mefahmam]
I don't understand.	**Ман намефаҳмам.** [man namefahmam]
Please speak more slowly.	**Лутфан, оҳиста гап занед.** [lutfan, ohista gap zaned]

| Is that correct? (Am I saying it right?) | **Ин дуруст?**
[in durust?] |
| What is this? (What does this mean?) | **Ин калима чӣ маъно дорад?**
[in kalima tʃi: ma'no dorad?] |

Apologies

Excuse me, please.	**Илтимос, бубахшед.** [iltimos, bubaxʃed]
I'm sorry.	**Афсӯс мехӯрам.** [afsœs meχœram]
I'm really sorry.	**Сад афсӯс.** [sad afsœs]
Sorry, it's my fault.	**Айби ман шуд.** [ajbi man ʃud]
My mistake.	**Хатои ман.** [χatoi man]
May I ...?	**Мумкин ман...** [mumkin man ...]
Do you mind if I ...?	**Агар зид набошед, ман ...** [agar zid naboʃed, man ...]
It's OK.	**Ҳеҷ гап не.** [heʤ gap ne]
It's all right.	**Ҳамааш дар ҷояш.** [hamaaʃ dar ʤojaʃ]
Don't worry about it.	**Ташвиш накашед.** [taʃviʃ nakaʃed]

Agreement

Yes.
Ҳа.
[ha]

Yes, sure.
Ҳа, албатта.
[ha, albatta]

OK (Good!)
Хуб!
[χub!]

Very well.
Хеле хуб!
[χele χub!]

Certainly!
Албатта!
[albatta!]

I agree.
Ман розӣ
[man rozi:]

That's correct.
Рост.
[rost]

That's right.
Дуруст.
[durust]

You're right.
Шумо ҳақ.
[ʃumo haq]

I don't mind.
Эътироз намекунам.
[e'tiroz namekunam]

Absolutely right.
Комилан дуруст.
[komilan durust]

It's possible.
Ин инконпазир аст.
[in inkonpazir ast]

That's a good idea.
Ин фикри хуб.
[in fikri χub]

I can't say no.
Не гуфта наметавонам.
[ne gufta nametavonam]

I'd be happy to.
Хурсанд мешавам.
[χursand meʃavam]

With pleasure.
Бо камоли майл.
[bo kamoli majl]

Refusal. Expressing doubt

No.
Не.
[ne]

Certainly not.
Албатта не.
[albatta ne]

I don't agree.
Ман розй не.
[man rozi: ne]

I don't think so.
Фикри ман дигар.
[fikri man digar]

It's not true.
Ин рост не.
[in rost ne]

You are wrong.
Шумо ҳақ нестед.
[ʃumo haq nested]

I think you are wrong.
Ба фикрам, ҳақ бар ҷониби шумо нест.
[ba fikram, haq bar dʒonibi ʃumo nest]

I'm not sure.
Дилпур нестам.
[dilpur nestam]

It's impossible.
Ин аз имкон берун аст.
[in az imkon berun ast]

Nothing of the kind (sort)!
Асло!
[aslo!]

The exact opposite.
Баръакс!
[bar'aks!]

I'm against it.
Ман зид.
[man zid]

I don't care.
Ба ман фарқ надорад.
[ba man farq nadorad]

I have no idea.
Хабар надорам.
[χabar nadoram]

I doubt it.
Аз ин шубҳа дорам.
[az in ʃubha doram]

Sorry, I can't.
Бубахшед, ман наметавонам.
[bubaχʃed, man nametavonam]

Sorry, I don't want to.
Бубахшед, ман намехоҳам.
[bubaχʃed, man nameχoham]

Thank you, but I don't need this.
Ташаккур, ин ба ман даркор не.
[taʃakkur, in ba man darkor ne]

It's getting late.
Хеле бевақт шуд.
[χele bevaqt ʃud]

I have to get up early.

Пагоҳ бояд барвақт хезам.
[pagoh bojad barvaqt χezam]

I don't feel well.

Худамро бад ҳис мекунам.
[χudamro bad his mekunam]

Expressing gratitude

Thank you.	**Ташаккур.** [taʃakkur]
Thank you very much.	**Ташаккури зиёд.** [taʃakkuri zijod]
I really appreciate it.	**Сипосгузорам.** [siposguzoram]
I'm really grateful to you.	**Аз шумо миннатдорам.** [az ʃumo minnatdoram]
We are really grateful to you.	**Аз шумо сипосгузорем.** [az ʃumo siposguzorem]
Thank you for your time.	**Ташаккур, ки вақт сарф кардед.** [taʃakkur, ki vaqt sarf karded.]
Thanks for everything.	**Ташаккур барои ҳама чиз.** [taʃakkur baroi hama tʃiz]
Thank you for ...	**Ташаккур барои ...** [taʃakkur baroi ...]
your help	**ёрии шумо** [jorii ʃumo]
a nice time	**вақти хуш** [vaqti χuʃ]
a wonderful meal	**хӯроки бомаза** [χœroki bomaza]
a pleasant evening	**шоми хуш** [ʃomi χuʃ]
a wonderful day	**рӯзи хотирмон** [rœzi χotirmon]
an amazing journey	**экскурсияи шавқовар** [ekskursijai ʃavqovar]
Don't mention it.	**Ҳеч гап не.** [hedʒ gap ne]
You are welcome.	**Намеарзад.** [namearzad]
Any time.	**Ҳамеша марҳамат.** [hameʃa marhamat]
My pleasure.	**Хушҳолам, ки кӯмак кардам.** [χuʃholam, ki kœmak kardam]
Forget it.	**Фаромӯш кунед. Ҳамааш дар ҷояш.** [faromœʃ kuned. hamaaʃ dar dʒojaʃ]
Don't worry about it.	**Ташвиш накашед.** [taʃviʃ nakaʃed]

Congratulations. Best wishes

Congratulations!

Табрик мекунам!
[tabrik mekunam!]

Happy birthday!

Зодрӯз муборак!
[zodrœz muborak!]

Merry Christmas!

Иди милод муборак!
[idi milod muborak!]

Happy New Year!

Соли нав муборак!
[soli nav muborak!]

Happy Easter!

Иди Песоҳ муборак!
[idi pesoh muborak!]

Happy Hanukkah!

Иди Ханука муборак!
[idi χanuka muborak!]

I'd like to propose a toast.

Нӯшбод дорам.
[nœʃbod doram]

Cheers!

Барои саломатии шумо!
[baroi salomatii ʃumo!]

Let's drink to …!

Барои ... менӯшем!
[baroi ... menœʃem!]

To our success!

Барои комёбии мо!
[baroi komjobii mo!]

To your success!

Барои комёбии шумо!
[baroi komjobii ʃumo!]

Good luck!

Муваффақият!
[muvaffaqijat!]

Have a nice day!

Рӯзи хуш!
[rœzi χuʃ!]

Have a good holiday!

Хуб дам гиред!
[χub dam gired!]

Have a safe journey!

Сафари хуш бод!
[safari χuʃ bod!]

I hope you get better soon!

Орзу мекунам, ки зудтар сиҳат шавед!
[orzu mekunam, ki zudtar sihat ʃaved!]

Socializing

Why are you sad?
Чаро озурда менамоед?
[tʃaro ozurda menamoed?]

Smile! Cheer up!
Табассум кунед!
[tabassum kuned!]

Are you free tonight?
Бегоҳӣ кор надоред?
[begohi: kor nadored?]

May I offer you a drink?
Мумкин ба шумо нӯшокӣ пешкаш кунам?
[mumkin ba ʃumo nœʃoki: peʃkaʃ kunam?]

Would you like to dance?
Рақс кардан намехоҳед?
[raqs kardan nameχohed?]

Let's go to the movies.
Шояд ба синамо равем?
[ʃojad ba sinamo ravem?]

May I invite you to …?
Мумкин шуморо ба … таклиф кунам?
[mumkin ʃumoro ba … taklif kunam?]

a restaurant
тарабхона
[tarabχona]

the movies
синамо
[sinamo]

the theater
театр
[teatr]

go for a walk
сайру гашт
[sajru gaʃt]

At what time?
Соати чанд?
[soati tʃand?]

tonight
имрӯз бегоҳӣ
[imrœz begohi:]

at six
дар соати шаш
[dar soati ʃaʃ]

at seven
дар соати ҳафт
[dar soati haft]

at eight
дар соати ҳашт
[dar soati haʃt]

at nine
дар соати нуҳ
[dar soati nuh]

Do you like it here?
Ба шумо ин ҷо маъқул?
[ba ʃumo in dʒo ma'qul?]

Are you here with someone?
Шумо дар ин ҷо танҳо?
[ʃumo dar in dʒo tanho?]

I'm with my friend.

Ман бо дӯстам /дугонаам/.
[man bo dœstam /dugonaam/]

I'm with my friends.

Ман бо дӯстонам.
[man bo dœstonam]

No, I'm alone.

Ман танҳо.
[man tanho]

Do you have a boyfriend?

Ту рафиқ дорӣ?
[tu rafiq dori:?]

I have a boyfriend.

Ман чӯра дорам.
[man dʒœra doram]

Do you have a girlfriend?

Ту дугона дорӣ?
[tu dugona dori:?]

I have a girlfriend.

Ман хонум дорам.
[man χonum doram]

Can I see you again?

Боз вомехӯрем?
[boz vomeχœrem?]

Can I call you?

Мумкин ба ту занг занам?
[mumkin ba tu zang zanam?]

Call me. (Give me a call.)

Ба ман занг зан.
[ba man zang zan]

What's your number?

Рақмат чанд?
[raqmat tʃand?]

I miss you.

Туро ёд мекунам.
[turo jod mekunam]

You have a beautiful name.

Номатон бисёр зебо.
[nomaton bisjor zebo]

I love you.

Ман туро дӯст медорам.
[man turo dœst medoram]

Will you marry me?

Ҳамсари ман шав.
[hamsari man ʃav]

You're kidding!

Шӯхӣ мекунед!
[ʃœχi: mekuned!]

I'm just kidding.

Ҳамту шӯхӣ буд.
[hamtu ʃœχi: bud]

Are you serious?

Шумо ҷиддӣ мегӯед?
[ʃumo dʒiddi: megœed?]

I'm serious.

Ман ҷиддӣ мегӯям.
[man dʒiddi: megœjam]

Really?!

Рост?!
[rost?!]

It's unbelievable!

Ин аз ақл берун!
[in az aql berun!]

I don't believe you.

Ман ба шумо бовар намекунам.
[man ba ʃumo bovar namekunam]

I can't.

Ман наметавонам.
[man nametavonam]

I don't know.

Ман намедонам.
[man namedonam]

I don't understand you.	**Ман шуморо намефаҳмам.** [man ʃumoro namefahmam]
Please go away.	**Лутафан, биравед.** [lutafan, biraved]
Leave me alone!	**Маро ташвиш надиҳед!** [maro taʃviʃ nadihed!]

I can't stand him.	**Ман вайро тоқати дидан надорам.** [man vajro toqati didan nadoram]
You are disgusting!	**Шумо нафратангез!** [ʃumo nafratangez!]
I'll call the police!	**Ман ба пулис занг мезанам!** [man ba pulis zang mezanam!]

Sharing impressions. Emotions

I like it.	**Ин ба ман маъқул.** [in ba man ma'qul]
Very nice.	**Хеле дилкаш.** [χele dilkaʃ]
That's great!	**Ин зӯр!** [in zœr!]
It's not bad.	**Ин бад не.** [in bad ne]
I don't like it.	**Ин ба ман маъқул не.** [in ba man ma'qul ne]
It's not good.	**Ин хуб не.** [in χub ne]
It's bad.	**Ин бад.** [in bad]
It's very bad.	**Ин хеле бад.** [in χele bad]
It's disgusting.	**Ин нафратангез.** [in nafratangez]
I'm happy.	**Ман хушбахт.** [man χuʃbaχt]
I'm content.	**Ман қаноатманд.** [man qanoatmand]
I'm in love.	**Ман ошиқ шудам.** [man oʃiq ʃudam]
I'm calm.	**Ман ором.** [man orom]
I'm bored.	**Дилгир шудам.** [dilgir ʃudam]
I'm tired.	**Монда шудам.** [monda ʃudam]
I'm sad.	**Зиқ шудам.** [ziq ʃudam]
I'm frightened.	**Ман метарсам.** [man metarsam]
I'm angry.	**Қаҳрам меояд.** [qahram meojad]
I'm worried.	**Ман дар ҳаяҷонам.** [man dar hajadʒonam]
I'm nervous.	**Асабонӣ мешавам.** [asaboni: meʃavam]

I'm jealous. (envious)	**Ман ҳасад мебарам.** [man hasad mebaram]
I'm surprised.	**Ман ҳайрон.** [man hajron]
I'm perplexed.	**Дар тааҷҷубам.** [dar taadʒdʒubam]

Problems. Accidents

I've got a problem.	**Ман мушкилӣ дорам.** [man muʃkili: doram]
We've got a problem.	**Мо мушкилӣ дорем.** [mo muʃkili: dorem]
I'm lost.	**Ман раҳгум задам.** [man rahgum zadam]
I missed the last bus (train).	**Ман ба автобуси (қатори) охирон дер кардам.** [man ba avtobusi (qatori) oχiron der kardam]
I don't have any money left.	**Ман тамоман бепул мондам.** [man tamoman bepul mondam]
I've lost my ...	**Ман ... гум кардам.** [man ... gum kardam]
Someone stole my ...	**... дуздиданд.** [... duzdidand]
passport	**шиносномаамро** [ʃinosnomaamro]
wallet	**ҳамёнамро** [hamjonamro]
papers	**ҳуҷҷатҳоямро** [hudʒdʒathojamro]
ticket	**чиптаамро** [tʃiptaamro]
money	**пулҳоямро** [pulhojamro]
handbag	**сумкаамро** [sumkaamro]
camera	**суратгиракамро** [suratgirakamro]
laptop	**ноутбукамро** [noutbukamro]
tablet computer	**планшетамро** [planʃetamro]
mobile phone	**телефонамро** [telefonamro]
Help me!	**Ёрӣ диҳед!** [jori: dihed!]
What's happened?	**Чӣ шуд?** [tʃi: ʃud?]

fire

сӯхтор
[sœxtor]

shooting

тирпаронӣ
[tirparoni:]

murder

куштор
[kuʃtor]

explosion

таркиш
[tarkiʃ]

fight

занозанӣ
[zanozani:]

Call the police!

Ба пулис занг занед!
[ba pulis zang zaned!]

Please hurry up!

Илтимос, зудтар!
[iltimos, zudtar!]

I'm looking for the police station.

Ман идораи пулис мекобам.
[man idorai pulis mekobam.]

I need to make a call.

Ба занг задан даркор.
[ba zang zadan darkor]

May I use your phone?

Мумкин занг занам?
[mumkin zang zanam?]

I've been ...

Маро
[maro]

mugged

ғорат карданд
[ğorat kardand]

robbed

дузд зад
[duzd zad]

raped

таҷовуз кардан
[taʤovuz kardan]

attacked (beaten up)

лату кӯб карданд
[latu kœb kardand]

Are you all right?

Ҳолатон хуб?
[holaton xub?]

Did you see who it was?

Шумо дидед, вай кӣ буд?
[ʃumo dided, vaj ki: bud?]

Would you be able to recognize
the person?

Вайро шинохта метавонед?
[vajro ʃinoxta metavoned?]

Are you sure?

Шумо аниқ медонед?
[ʃumo aniq medoned?]

Please calm down.

Илтимос, ором шавед.
[iltimos, orom ʃaved]

Take it easy!

Ором!
[orom!]

Don't worry!

Ташвиш накашед.
[taʃviʃ nakaʃed]

Everything will be fine.

Ҳамааш хуб мешавад.
[hamaaʃ xub meʃavad]

Everything's all right.

Ҳамааш дар ҷояш.
[hamaaʃ dar ʤojaʃ]

Come here, please.

Лутфан, наздик оед.
[lutfan, nazdik oed]

I have some questions for you.

Ба шумо якчанд савол дорам.
[ba ʃumo jaktʃand savol doram]

Wait a moment, please.

Лутфан, мунтазир шавед.
[lutfan, muntazir ʃaved]

Do you have any I.D.?

Шумо ҳуҷҷат доред?
[ʃumo hudʒdʒat dored?]

Thanks. You can leave now.

Ташаккур. Шумо рафта метавонед.
[taʃakkur. ʃumo rafta metavoned]

Hands behind your head!

Дастҳо пушти сар!
[dastho puʃti sar!]

You're under arrest!

Шумо ҳабс шудед!
[ʃumo habs ʃuded!]

Health problems

Please help me.
Лутфан, ёрй диҳед.
[lutfan, jori: dihed]

I don't feel well.
Худамро бад ҳис мекунам.
[χudamro bad his mekunam]

My husband doesn't feel well.
Ҳоли шавҳарам бад шуд.
[holi ʃavharam bad ʃud]

My son …
Ҳоли писарам …
[holi pisaram …]

My father …
Ҳоли падарам …
[holi padaram …]

My wife doesn't feel well.
Ҳоли занам бад шуд.
[holi zanam bad ʃud]

My daughter …
Ҳоли духтарам …
[holi duχtaram …]

My mother …
Ҳоли модарам …
[holi modaram …]

I've got a …
… дард мекунад.
[… dard mekunad]

headache
сарам
[saram]

sore throat
гулӯям
[gulœjam]

stomach ache
шикамам
[ʃikamam]

toothache
дандонам
[dandonam]

I feel dizzy.
Сарам тоб мехӯрад.
[saram tob meχœrad]

He has a fever.
Тафс дорам.
[tafs doram]

She has a fever.
Вай тафс дорад.
[vaj tafs dorad]

I can't breathe.
Нафас кашида наметавонам.
[nafas kaʃida nametavonam]

I'm short of breath.
Нафасгир мешавам.
[nafasgir meʃavam]

I am asthmatic.
Ман астма дорам.
[man astma doram]

I am diabetic.
Ман қандкасалам.
[man qandkasalam]

I can't sleep.	**Бедорхобӣ мекашам.** [bedorχobi: mekaʃam]
food poisoning	**Заҳролудшавии ғизой** [zahroludʃavii ğizoi:]

It hurts here.	**Ин ҷоям дард мекунад.** [in dʒojam dard mekunad]
Help me!	**Ёрӣ диҳед!** [jori: dihed!]
I am here!	**Ман ҳамин ҷо!** [man hamin dʒo!]
We are here!	**Мо ҳамин ҷо!** [mo hamin dʒo!]
Get me out of here!	**Маро кашида бароред!** [maro kaʃida barored!]
I need a doctor.	**Ба ман духтур даркор.** [ba man duχtur darkor]
I can't move.	**Ҳаракат карда наметавонам.** [harakat karda nametavonam]
I can't move my legs.	**Пойҳоямро ҳис намекунам.** [pojhojamro his namekunam]

I have a wound.	**Ман захм хӯрдам.** [man zaχm χœrdam]
Is it serious?	**Ин ҷиддӣ?** [in dʒiddi:?]
My documents are in my pocket.	**Хуҷҷатҳоям дар киса.** [hudʒdʒathojam dar kisa]
Calm down!	**Ором шавед!** [orom ʃaved!]
May I use your phone?	**Мумкин занг занам?** [mumkin zang zanam?]

Call an ambulance!	**Ба ёрии таъҷилӣ занг занед!** [ba jorii ta'dʒili: zang zaned!]
It's urgent!	**Ин фаврӣ!** [in favri:!]
It's an emergency!	**Ин бисёр фаврӣ!** [in bisjor favri:!]
Please hurry up!	**Илтимос, зудтар!** [iltimos, zudtar!]
Would you please call a doctor?	**Илтимос, духтурро ҷеғ занед.** [iltimos, duχturro dʒeğ zaned]
Where is the hospital?	**Беморохона дар куҷо?** [bemoroχona dar kudʒo?]

How are you feeling?	**Худро чи хел ҳис мекунед?** [χudro tʃi χel his mekuned?]
Are you all right?	**Ҳолатон хуб?** [holaton χub?]
What's happened?	**Чӣ рӯй дод?** [tʃi: rœj dod?]

I feel better now.

Аллакай, худро беҳтар ҳис мекунам.
[allakaj, χudro behtar his mekunam]

It's OK.

Ҳамааш дар чояш.
[hamaaʃ dar dʒojaʃ]

It's all right.

Ҳамааш хуб.
[hamaaʃ χub]

At the pharmacy

pharmacy (drugstore)	**дорухона** [doruxona]
24-hour pharmacy	**дорухонаи шабонарӯзӣ** [doruxonai ʃabonarœzi:]
Where is the closest pharmacy?	**Дорухонаи наздиктарин дар кучо?** [doruxonai nazdiktarin dar kudʒo?]
Is it open now?	**Ҳоло кушода аст?** [holo kuʃoda ast?]
At what time does it open?	**Соати чанд кушода мешавад?** [soati tʃand kuʃoda meʃavad?]
At what time does it close?	**То соати чанд кор мекунад?** [to soati tʃand kor mekunad?]
Is it far?	**Ин дур аст?** [in dur ast?]
Can I get there on foot?	**Ба ончо пиёда рафта метавонам?** [ba ondʒo pijoda rafta metavonam?]
Can you show me on the map?	**Илтимос, дар харита нишон диҳед.** [iltimos, dar xarita niʃon dihed]
Please give me something for ...	**Ба ман ягон чиз аз ... диҳед.** [ba man jagon tʃiz az ... dihed]
a headache	**дарди сар** [dardi sar]
a cough	**сулфа** [sulfa]
a cold	**шамолхӯрӣ** [ʃamolxœri:]
the flu	**зуком** [zukom]
a fever	**тафс** [tafs]
a stomach ache	**дарди меъда** [dardi me'da]
nausea	**дилбеҳузурӣ** [dilbehuzuri:]
diarrhea	**шикамравӣ** [ʃikamravi:]
constipation	**қабзият** [qabzijat]
pain in the back	**дарди миён** [dardi mijon]

chest pain
дарди қафаси сина
[dardi qafasi sina]

side stitch
дарди паҳлӯ
[dardi pahlœ]

abdominal pain
дарди шикам
[dardi ʃikam]

pill
доруи ҳаб
[dorui hab]

ointment, cream
марҳам, крем
[marham, krem]

syrup
шира
[ʃira]

spray
спрей
[sprej]

drops
чакрагӣ
[tʃakragi:]

You need to go to the hospital.
Шумо бояд ба беморхона равед.
[ʃumo bojad ba bemorχona raved]

health insurance
таъминот
[ta'minot]

prescription
ретсепт
[retsept]

insect repellant
доруи ҳашарот
[dorui haʃarot]

Band Aid
часпи захм
[tʃaspi zaχm]

The bare minimum

Excuse me, ...
Бубахшед, ...
[bubaχ∫ed, ...]

Hello.
Салом.
[salom]

Thank you.
Ташаккур.
[ta∫akkur]

Good bye.
То дидан.
[to didan]

Yes.
Ҳа.
[ha]

No.
Не.
[ne]

I don't know.
Ман намедонам.
[man namedonam]

Where? | Where to? | When?
Дар куҷо? | Ба куҷо? | Кай?
[dar kuʤo? | ba kuʤo? | kaj?]

I need ...
Ба ман ... даркор аст.
[ba man ... darkor ast]

I want ...
Ман ... мехоҳам.
[man ... meχoham]

Do you have ...?
Шумо ... доред?
[∫umo ... dored?]

Is there a ... here?
Дар ин ҷо ... ҳаст?
[dar in ʤo ... hast?]

May I ...?
... метавонам?
[... metavonam?]

..., please (polite request)
Илтимос
[iltimos]

I'm looking for ...
Ман ... мекобам.
[man ... mekobam]

restroom
хоҷатхона
[χoʤatχona]

ATM
худпардоз
[χudpardoz]

pharmacy (drugstore)
дорухона
[doruχona]

hospital
беморхона
[bemorχona]

police station
идораи пулис
[idorai pulis]

subway
метро
[metro]

taxi	**такси** [taksi]
train station	**вокзал** [vokzal]

My name is …	**Номи ман …** [nomi man …]
What's your name?	**Номи шумо чӣ?** [nomi ʃumo tʃi:?]
Could you please help me?	**Илтимос, ба ман ёрӣ диҳед.** [iltimos, ba man jori: dihed]
I've got a problem.	**Ман мушкилӣ дорам.** [man muʃkili: doram]
I don't feel well.	**Худамро бад ҳис мекунам.** [χudamro bad his mekunam]
Call an ambulance!	**Ба ёрии таъчилӣ занг занед!** [ba jorii ta'dʒili: zang zaned!]
May I make a call?	**Мумкин занг занам?** [mumkin zang zanam?]

I'm sorry.	**Бубахшед** [bubaχʃed]
You're welcome.	**Намеарзад** [namearzad]

I, me	**ман** [man]
you (inform.)	**ту** [tu]
he	**ӯ, вай** [œ, vaj]
she	**ӯ, вай** [œ, vaj]
they (masc.)	**онҳо** [onho]
they (fem.)	**онҳо** [onho]
we	**мо** [mo]
you (pl)	**шумо** [ʃumo]
you (sg, form.)	**Шумо** [ʃumo]

ENTRANCE	**ДАРОМАДГОҲ** [daromadgoh]
EXIT	**БАРОМАДГОҲ** [baromadgoh]
OUT OF ORDER	**КОР НАМЕКУНАД** [kor namekunad]
CLOSED	**ПӮШИДА** [pœʃida]

OPEN   **КУШОДА**
[kuʃoda]

FOR WOMEN   **БАРОИ ЗАНОН**
[baroi zanon]

FOR MEN   **БАРОИ МАРДОН**
[baroi mardon]

CONCISE DICTIONARY

This section contains more than 1,500 useful words arranged alphabetically. The dictionary includes a lot of gastronomic terms and will be helpful when ordering food at a restaurant or buying groceries

T&P Books Publishing

DICTIONARY CONTENTS

T&P Books Publishing

1. Time. Calendar

time	вақт	[vaqt]
hour	соат	[soat]
half an hour	нимсоат	[nimsoat]
minute	дақиқа	[daqiqa]
second	сония	[sonija]
today (adv)	имрӯз	[imrœz]
tomorrow (adv)	пагоҳ, фардо	[pagoh], [fardo]
yesterday (adv)	дирӯз, дина	[dirœz], [dina]
Monday	душанбе	[duʃanbe]
Tuesday	сешанбе	[seʃanbe]
Wednesday	чоршанбе	[ʧorʃanbe]
Thursday	панҷшанбе	[panʤʃanbe]
Friday	ҷумъа	[ʤum'a]
Saturday	шанбе	[ʃanbe]
Sunday	якшанбе	[jakʃanbe]
day	рӯз	[rœz]
working day	рӯзи кор	[rœzi kor]
public holiday	рӯзи ид	[rœzi id]
weekend	рӯзҳои истироҳат	[rœzhoi istirohat]
week	ҳафта	[hafta]
last week (adv)	ҳафтаи гузашта	[haftai guzaʃta]
next week (adv)	ҳафтаи оянда	[haftai ojanda]
sunrise	тулӯъ	[tulœ']
sunset	ғуруби офтоб	[ʁurubi oftob]
in the morning	пагоҳирӯзй	[pagohirœzi:]
in the afternoon	баъди пешин	[ba'di peʃin]
in the evening	бегоҳй, бегоҳирӯзй	[begohi:], [begohirœzi:]
tonight (this evening)	ҳамин бегоҳ	[hamin begoh]
at night	шабона	[ʃabona]
midnight	нисфи шаб	[nisfi ʃab]
January	январ	[janvar]
February	феврал	[fevral]
March	март	[mart]
April	апрел	[aprel]
May	май	[maj]
June	июн	[ijun]

July	июл	[ijul]
August	август	[avgust]
September	сентябр	[sentjabr]
October	октябр	[oktjabr]
November	ноябр	[nojabr]
December	декабр	[dekabr]

in spring	дар фасли баҳор	[dar fasli bahor]
in summer	дар тобистон	[dar tobiston]
in fall	дар тирамоҳ	[dar tiramoh]
in winter	дар зимистон	[dar zimiston]

month	моҳ	[moh]
season (summer, etc.)	фасл	[fasl]
year	сол	[sol]
century	аср	[asr]

2. Numbers. Numerals

digit, figure	рақам	[raqam]
number	адад	[adad]
minus sign	тарҳ	[tarh]
plus sign	ҷамъ	[dʒam']
sum, total	ҳосили ҷамъ	[hosili dʒam']

first (adj)	якум	[jakum]
second (adj)	дуюм	[dujum]
third (adj)	сеюм	[sejum]

0 zero	сифр	[sifr]
1 one	як	[jak]
2 two	ду	[du]
3 three	се	[se]
4 four	чор, чаҳор	[tʃor], [tʃahor]

5 five	панҷ	[pandʒ]
6 six	шаш	[ʃaʃ]
7 seven	ҳафт	[haft]
8 eight	ҳашт	[haʃt]
9 nine	нуҳ	[nuh]
10 ten	даҳ	[dah]

11 eleven	ёздаҳ	[jozdah]
12 twelve	дувоздаҳ	[duvozdah]
13 thirteen	сездаҳ	[sezdah]
14 fourteen	чордаҳ	[tʃordah]
15 fifteen	понздаҳ	[ponzdah]

16 sixteen	шонздаҳ	[ʃonzdah]
17 seventeen	ҳафдаҳ	[hafdah]

| 18 eighteen | ҳаждаҳ | [haʒdah] |
| 19 nineteen | нуздаҳ | [nuzdah] |

20 twenty	бист	[bist]
30 thirty	сӣ	[si:]
40 forty	чил	[tʃil]
50 fifty	панҷоҳ	[pandʒoh]

60 sixty	шаст	[ʃast]
70 seventy	ҳафтод	[haftod]
80 eighty	ҳаштод	[haʃtod]
90 ninety	навад	[navad]

100 one hundred	сад	[sad]
200 two hundred	дусад	[dusad]
300 three hundred	сесад	[sesad]
400 four hundred	чорсад, чаҳорсад	[tʃorsad], [tʃahorsad]
500 five hundred	панҷсад	[pandʒsad]

600 six hundred	шашсад	[ʃaʃsad]
700 seven hundred	ҳафтсад	[haftsad]
800 eight hundred	ҳаштсад	[haʃtsad]
900 nine hundred	нӯҳсадум	[nœhsadum]
1000 one thousand	ҳазор	[hazor]

| 10000 ten thousand | даҳ ҳазор | [dah hazor] |
| one hundred thousand | сад ҳазор | [sad hazor] |

| million | миллион | [million] |
| billion | миллиард | [milliard] |

3. Humans. Family

man (adult male)	мард	[mard]
young man	ҷавон	[dʒavon]
teenager	наврас	[navras]
woman	зан, занак	[zan], [zanak]
girl (young woman)	ҷавондухтар	[dʒavonduχtar]

age	син	[sin]
adult (adj)	калонсол	[kalonsol]
middle-aged (adj)	солдида	[soldida]
elderly (adj)	пир, солхӯрда	[pir], [solχœrda]
old (adj)	пир	[pir]

old man	пир	[pir]
old woman	пиразан	[pirazan]
retirement	нафақа	[nafaqa]
to retire (from job)	ба нафақа баромадан	[ba nafaqa baromadan]
retiree	нафақахӯр	[nafaqaχœr]

mother	модар	[modar]
father	падар	[padar]
son	писар	[pisar]
daughter	духтар	[duχtar]
brother	бародар	[barodar]
elder brother	ака	[aka]
younger brother	додар	[dodar]
sister	хоҳар	[χohar]
elder sister	апа	[apa]
younger sister	хоҳари хурд	[χohari χurd]

parents	волидайн	[volidajn]
child	кӯдак	[kœdak]
children	бачагон, кӯдакон	[batʃagon], [kœdakon]
stepmother	модарандар	[modarandar]
stepfather	падарандар	[padarandar]

grandmother	модаркалон, онакалон	[modarkalon], [onakalon]
grandfather	бобо	[bobo]
grandson	набера	[nabera]
granddaughter	набера	[nabera]
grandchildren	набераҳо	[naberaho]

uncle	таго, амак	[taʁo], [amak]
aunt	хола, амма	[χola], [amma]
nephew	ҷиян	[dʒijan]
niece	ҷиян	[dʒijan]

wife	зан	[zan]
husband	шавҳар, шӯй	[ʃavhar], [ʃœj]
married (masc.)	зандор	[zandor]
married (fem.)	шавҳардор	[ʃavhardor]
widow	бева, бевазан	[beva], [bevazan]
widower	бева, занмурда	[beva], [zanmurda]

| name (first name) | ном | [nom] |
| surname (last name) | фамилия | [familija] |

relative	хеш	[χeʃ]
friend (masc.)	дӯст, ҷӯра	[dœst], [dʒœra]
friendship	дӯстӣ, ҷӯрагӣ	[dœsti:], [dʒœragi:]
partner	шарик	[ʃarik]
superior (n)	сардор	[sardor]
colleague	ҳамкор	[hamkor]
neighbors	ҳамсояҳо	[hamsojaho]

4. Human body

| organism (body) | организм | [organizm] |
| body | бадан | [badan] |

heart	дил	[dil]
blood	хун	[χun]
brain	мағз	[maʁz]
nerve	асаб	[asab]

bone	устухон	[ustuχon]
skeleton	устухонбандӣ	[ustuχonbandi:]
spine (backbone)	сутунмӯхра	[sutunmœhra]
rib	кабурға	[kaburʁa]
skull	косаи сар	[kosai sar]

muscle	мушак	[muʃak]
lungs	шуш	[ʃuʃ]
skin	пӯст	[pœst]

head	сар	[sar]
face	рӯй	[rœj]
nose	бинӣ	[bini:]
forehead	пешона	[peʃona]
cheek	рухсор	[ruχsor]

mouth	даҳон	[dahon]
tongue	забон	[zabon]
tooth	дандон	[dandon]
lips	лабҳо	[labho]
chin	манаҳ	[manah]

ear	гӯш	[gœʃ]
neck	гардан	[gardan]
throat	гулӯ	[gulœ]

eye	чашм, дида	[tʃaʃm], [dida]
pupil	гавҳараки чашм	[gavharaki tʃaʃm]
eyebrow	абрӯ, қош	[abrœ], [qoʃ]
eyelash	мижа	[miʒa]

hair	мӯйи сар	[mœji sar]
hairstyle	ороиши мӯйсар	[oroiʃi mœjsar]
mustache	муйлаб, бурут	[mujlab], [burut]
beard	риш	[riʃ]
to have (a beard, etc.)	мондан, доштан	[mondan], [doʃtan]
bald (adj)	одамсар	[odamsar]

hand	панҷаи даст	[pandʒai dast]
arm	даст	[dast]
finger	ангушт	[anguʃt]
nail	нохун	[noχun]
palm	каф	[kaf]

shoulder	китф	[kitf]
leg	по	[po]
foot	панҷаи пой	[pandʒai poj]

| knee | зону | [zonu] |
| heel | пошна | [poʃna] |

back	пушт	[puʃt]
waist	миён	[mijon]
beauty mark	хол	[χol]
birthmark (café au lait spot)	хол	[χol]

5. Medicine. Diseases. Drugs

health	тандурустӣ, саломатӣ	[tandurusti:], [salomati:]
well (not sick)	тандуруст	[tandurust]
sickness	касалӣ, беморӣ	[kasali:], [bemori:]
to be sick	бемор будан	[bemor budan]
ill, sick (adj)	касал, бемор	[kasal], [bemor]

cold (illness)	шамол хӯрдани	[ʃamol χœrdani]
to catch a cold	шамол хӯрдан	[ʃamol χœrdan]
tonsillitis	дарди гулӯ	[dardi gulœ]
pneumonia	варами шуш	[varami ʃuʃ]
flu, influenza	грипп	[gripp]

runny nose (coryza)	зуком	[zukom]
cough	сулфа	[sulfa]
to cough (vi)	сулфидан	[sulfidan]
to sneeze (vi)	атса задан	[atsa zadan]

stroke	сактаи майна	[saktai majna]
heart attack	инфаркт, сактаи дил	[infarkt], [saktai dil]
allergy	аллергия	[allergija]
asthma	астма, зиққи нафас	[astma], [ziqqi nafas]
diabetes	диабет	[diabet]

tumor	варам	[varam]
cancer	саратон	[saraton]
alcoholism	майзадагӣ	[majzadagi:]
AIDS	СПИД	[spid]
fever	табларза, варача	[tablarza], [varadʒa]
seasickness	касалии бахр	[kasali:i bahr]

bruise (hématome)	доғи кабуд, кабудӣ	[doʁi kabud], [kabudi:]
bump (lump)	ғуррӣ	[ʁurri:]
to limp (vi)	лангидан	[langidan]
dislocation	баромадан	[baromadan]
to dislocate (vt)	баровардан	[barovardan]

fracture	шикасти устухон	[ʃikasti ustuχon]
burn (injury)	сӯхта	[sœχta]
injury	захм	[zaχm]

| pain, ache | дард | [dard] |
| toothache | дарди дандон | [dardi dandon] |

to sweat (perspire)	арақ кардан	[araq kardan]
deaf (adj)	кар, гӯшкар	[kar], [gœʃkar]
mute (adj)	гунг	[gung]

immunity	сироятнопазирӣ	[sirojatnopaziri:]
virus	вирус	[virus]
microbe	микроб	[mikrob]
bacterium	бактерия	[bakterija]
infection	сироят	[sirojat]

hospital	касалхона	[kasalχona]
cure	муолиҷа	[muoliʤa]
to vaccinate (vt)	эмгузаронӣ кардан	[ɛmguzaroni: kardan]
to be in a coma	дар кома будан	[dar koma budan]
intensive care	шӯъбаи эҳё	[ʃœ'bai ɛhjɔ]
symptom	аломат	[alomat]
pulse	набз	[nabz]

6. Feelings. Emotions. Conversation

I, me	ман	[man]
you	ту	[tu]
he	ӯ, вай	[œ], [vaj]
she	ӯ, вай	[œ], [vaj]
it	он	[on]

we	мо	[mo]
you (to a group)	шумо	[ʃumo]
you (polite, sing.)	Шумо	[ʃumo]
you (polite, pl)	Шумо	[ʃumo]
they (inanim.)	онон	[onon]
they (anim.)	онҳо, вайҳо	[onho], [vajho]

Hello! (fam.)	Салом!	[salom]
Hello! (form.)	Ассалом!	[assalom]
Good morning!	Субҳатон ба хайр!	[subhaton ba χajr]
Good afternoon!	Рӯз ба хайр!	[rœz ba χajr]
Good evening!	Шом ба хайр!	[ʃom ba χajr]

to say hello	саломалейк кардан	[salomalejk kardan]
to greet (vt)	вохӯрдӣ кардан	[voχœrdi: kardan]
How are you? (form.)	Корхоятон чӣ хел?	[korhojaton tʃi: χel]
How are you? (fam.)	Корхоят чӣ хел?	[korhojat tʃi: χel]
Goodbye! (form.)	То дидан!	[to didan]
Bye! (fam.)	Хайр!	[χajr]
Thank you!	Раҳмат!	[rahmat]
feelings	ҳиссиёт	[hissijɔt]

to be hungry	хӯрок хостан	[xœrok xostan]
to be thirsty	об хостан	[ob xostan]
tired (adj)	мондашуда	[mondaʃuda]

to be worried	нороҳат шудан	[norohat ʃudan]
to be nervous	асабони шудан	[asaboni ʃudan]
hope	умед	[umed]
to hope (vi, vt)	умед доштан	[umed doʃtan]

character	феъл, табиат	[fe'l], [tabiat]
modest (adj)	хоксор	[xoksor]
lazy (adj)	танбал	[tanbal]
generous (adj)	сахӣ	[saxi:]
talented (adj)	боистеъдод	[boiste'dod]

honest (adj)	бовиҷдон	[bovidʒdon]
serious (adj)	мулоҳизакор	[mulohizakor]
shy, timid (adj)	беҷуръат	[bedʒur'at]
sincere (adj)	самимӣ	[samimi:]
coward	тарсончак	[tarsontʃak]

to sleep (vi)	хобидан	[xobidan]
dream	хоб	[xob]
bed	кат	[kat]
pillow	болишт	[boliʃt]

insomnia	бехобӣ	[bexobi:]
to go to bed	хобравӣ рафтан	[xobravi: raftan]
nightmare	сиёҳӣ	[sijohi:]
alarm clock	соати рӯимизии зангдор	[soati rœimizi:i zangdor]

smile	табассум	[tabassum]
to smile (vi)	табассум кардан	[tabassum kardan]
to laugh (vi)	хандидан	[xandidan]

quarrel	ҷанҷол	[dʒandʒol]
insult	таҳқир	[tahqir]
resentment	озор, озурдаги	[ozor], [ozurdagi]
angry (mad)	бадқаҳр	[badqahr]

7. Clothing. Personal accessories

clothes	либос	[libos]
coat (overcoat)	палто	[palto]
fur coat	пӯстин	[pœstin]
jacket (e.g., leather ~)	куртка	[kurtka]
raincoat (trenchcoat, etc.)	боронӣ	[boroni:]
shirt (button shirt)	курта	[kurta]
pants	шим, шалвор	[ʃim], [ʃalvor]

| suit jacket | пиҷак | [piʤak] |
| suit | костюм | [kostjum] |

dress (frock)	куртаи заннона	[kurtai zannona]
skirt	юбка	[jubka]
T-shirt	футболка	[futbolka]
bathrobe	халат	[χalat]
pajamas	пижама	[piʒama]
workwear	либоси корй	[libosi kori:]

underwear	либоси таг	[libosi tag]
socks	пайпоқ	[pajpoq]
bra	синабанд	[sinaband]
pantyhose	колготка	[kolgotka]
stockings (thigh highs)	чуроби дароз	[ʧurobi daroz]
bathing suit	либоси оббозй	[libosi obbozi:]

hat	кулоҳ, телпак	[kuloh], [telpak]
footwear	пойафзол	[pojafzol]
boots (e.g., cowboy ~)	мӯза	[mœza]
heel	пошна	[poʃna]
shoestring	бандак	[bandak]
shoe polish	креми пойафзол	[kremi pojafzol]

cotton (n)	пахта	[paχta]
wool (n)	пашм	[paʃm]
fur (n)	мӯина, пӯст	[mœina], [pœst]

gloves	дастпӯшак	[dastpœʃak]
mittens	дастпӯшаки бепанҷа	[dastpœʃaki bepanʤa]
scarf (muffler)	гарданпеч	[gardanpeʧ]
glasses (eyeglasses)	айнак	[ajnak]
umbrella	соябон, чатр	[sojabon], [ʧatr]

tie (necktie)	галстук	[galstuk]
handkerchief	дастрӯймол	[dastrœjmol]
comb	шона	[ʃona]
hairbrush	чӯткаи мӯйсар	[ʧœtkai mœjsar]

buckle	сагаки тасма	[sagaki tasma]
belt	тасма	[tasma]
purse	сумка	[sumka]

collar	гиребон, ёқа	[girebon], [jɔqa]
pocket	киса	[kisa]
sleeve	остин	[ostin]
fly (on trousers)	чоки пеши шим	[ʧoki peʃi ʃim]

zipper (fastener)	занҷирак	[zanʤirak]
button	тугма	[tugma]
to get dirty (vi)	олуда шудан	[oluda ʃudan]
stain (mark, spot)	доғ, лакка	[doʁ], [lakka]

8. City. Urban institutions

store	магазин	[magazin]
shopping mall	маркази савдо	[markazi savdo]
supermarket	супермаркет	[supermarket]
shoe store	магазини пойафзолфурӯшӣ	[magazini pojafzolfurœʃi:]
bookstore	мағозаи китоб	[maʁozai kitob]
drugstore, pharmacy	дорухона	[doruχona]
bakery	дӯкони нонфурӯшӣ	[dœkoni nonfurœʃi:]
pastry shop	қаннодӣ	[qannodi:]
grocery store	дӯкони баққолӣ	[dœkoni baqqoli:]
butcher shop	дӯкони гӯштфурӯшӣ	[dœkoni gœʃtfurœʃi:]
produce store	дӯкони сабзавот	[dœkoni sabzavot]
market	бозор	[bozor]
hair salon	сартарошхона	[sartaroʃχona]
post office	пӯшта	[pœʃta]
dry cleaners	козургарии химиявӣ	[kozurgari:i χimijavi:]
circus	сирк	[sirk]
zoo	боғи ҳайвонот	[boʁi hajvonot]
theater	театр	[teatr]
movie theater	кинотеатр	[kinoteatr]
museum	осорхона	[osorχona]
library	китобхона	[kitobχona]
mosque	масҷид	[masdʒid]
synagogue	каниса	[kanisa]
cathedral	собор	[sobor]
temple	ибодатгоҳ	[ibodatgoh]
church	калисо	[kaliso]
college	институт	[institut]
university	университет	[universitet]
school	мактаб	[maktab]
hotel	меҳмонхона	[mehmonχona]
bank	банк	[bank]
embassy	сафорат	[saforat]
travel agency	турагенство	[turagenstvo]
subway	метро	[metro]
hospital	касалхона	[kasalχona]
gas station	нуқтаи фурӯши сӯзишворӣ	[nuqtai furœʃi sœziʃvori:]
parking lot	истгоҳи мошинҳо	[istgohi moʃinho]
ENTRANCE	ДАРОМАД	[daromad]
EXIT	БАРОМАД	[baromad]

PUSH	АЗ ХУД	[az χud]
PULL	БА ХУД	[ba χud]
OPEN	КУШОДА	[kuʃoda]
CLOSED	ПӮШИДА	[pœʃida]

monument	ҳайкал	[hajkal]
fortress	ҳисор	[hisor]
palace	қаср	[qasr]

medieval (adj)	асримиёнагӣ	[asrimijɔnagi:]
ancient (adj)	қадим	[qadim]
national (adj)	миллӣ	[milli:]
famous (monument, etc.)	маъруф	[ma'ruf]

9. Money. Finances

money	пул	[pul]
coin	танга	[tanga]
dollar	доллар	[dollar]
ATM	банкомат	[bankomat]
currency exchange	нуқтаи мубодила	[nuqtai mubodila]
exchange rate	қурб	[qurb]
cash	пули нақд, нақдина	[puli naqd], [naqdina]

How much?	Чанд пул?	[tʃand pul]
to pay (vi, vt)	пул додан	[pul dodan]
payment	пардохт	[pardoχt]
change (give the ~)	бақияи пул	[baqijai pul]

price	нарх	[narχ]
discount	тахфиф	[taχfif]
cheap (adj)	арзон	[arzon]
expensive (adj)	қимат	[qimat]

bank	банк	[bank]
account	ҳисоб	[hisob]
credit card	корти кредитӣ	[korti krediti:]
check	чек	[tʃek]
to write a check	чек навиштан	[tʃek naviʃtan]
checkbook	дафтарчаи чек	[daftartʃai tʃek]

debt	қарз	[qarz]
debtor	қарздор	[qarzdor]
to lend (money)	қарз додан	[qarz dodan]
to borrow (vi, vt)	қарз гирифтан	[qarz giriftan]

to rent (~ a tuxedo)	насия гирифтан	[nasija giriftan]
on credit (adv)	кредит гирифтан	[kredit giriftan]
wallet	ҳамён	[hamjɔn]
safe	сейф	[sejf]

| inheritance | мерос | [meros] |
| fortune (wealth) | дорой | [doroi:] |

tax	налог, андоз	[nalog], [andoz]
fine	чарима	[ʤarima]
to fine (vt)	чарима андохтан	[ʤarima andoχtan]

wholesale (adj)	кӯтара, яклухт	[kœtara], [jakluχt]
retail (adj)	чакана	[ʧakana]
to insure (vt)	суғурта кардан	[suʁurta kardan]
insurance	суғурта	[suʁurta]

capital	капитал	[kapital]
turnover	гардиш	[gardiʃ]
stock (share)	саҳмия	[sahmija]
profit	даромад, фоида	[daromad], [foida]
profitable (adj)	фоиданок	[foidanok]

crisis	бӯҳрон	[bœhron]
bankruptcy	шикаст, муфлисӣ	[ʃikast], [muflisi:]
to go bankrupt	муфлис шудан	[muflis ʃudan]

accountant	бухгалтер	[buχʁalter]
salary	музди меҳнат	[muzdi mehnat]
bonus (money)	чоиза	[ʤoiza]

10. Transportation

bus	автобус	[avtobus]
streetcar	трамвай	[tramvaj]
trolley bus	троллейбус	[trollejbus]

to go by ...	савор будан	[savor budan]
to get on (~ the bus)	савор шудан	[savor ʃudan]
to get off ...	фуромадан	[furomadan]

stop (e.g., bus ~)	истгоҳ	[istgoh]
terminus	истгоҳи охирон	[istgohi oχiron]
schedule	чадвал	[ʤadval]
ticket	билет	[bilet]
to be late (for ...)	дер мондан	[der mondan]

taxi, cab	такси	[taksi]
by taxi	дар такси	[dar taksi]
taxi stand	истгоҳи таксӣ	[istgohi taksi:]

traffic	ҳаракат дар кӯча	[harakat dar kœʧa]
rush hour	час пик	[ʧas pik]
to park (vi)	чой кардан	[ʤoj kardan]
subway	метро	[metro]

station	истгоҳ	[istgoh]
train	поезд, қатор	[poezd], [qator]
train station	вокзал	[vokzal]
rails	релсхо	[relsho]
compartment	купе	[kupe]
berth	кат	[kat]

airplane	ҳавопаймо	[havopajmo]
air ticket	чиптаи ҳавопаймо	[tʃiptai havopajmo]
airline	ширкати ҳавопаймой	[ʃirkati havopajmoi:]
airport	аэропорт	[aɛroport]

flight (act of flying)	парвоз	[parvoz]
luggage	бағоҷ, бор	[baʁodʒ], [bor]
luggage cart	аробаи боғочкашй	[arobai boʁotʃkaʃi:]

ship	киштй	[kiʃti:]
cruise ship	лайнер	[lajner]
yacht	яхта	[jaχta]
boat (flat-bottomed ~)	қаиқ	[qaiq]

captain	капитан	[kapitan]
cabin	каюта	[kajuta]
port (harbor)	бандар	[bandar]

bicycle	велосипед	[velosiped]
scooter	мотороллер	[motoroller]
motorcycle, bike	мотосикл	[motosikl]
pedal	педал	[pedal]
pump	насос	[nasos]
wheel	чарх	[tʃarχ]

automobile, car	автомобил	[avtomobil]
ambulance	ёрии таъҷилй	[jori:i ta'dʒili:]
truck	мошини боркаш	[moʃini borkaʃ]
used (adj)	нимдошт	[nimdoʃt]
car crash	садама	[sadama]
repair	таъмир	[ta'mir]

11. Food. Part 1

meat	гӯшт	[gœʃt]
chicken	мурғ	[murʁ]
duck	мурғобӣ	[murʁobi:]
pork	гӯшти хук	[gœʃti χuk]
veal	гӯшти гӯсола	[gœʃti gœsola]
lamb	гӯшти гӯсфанд	[gœʃti gœsfand]
beef	гӯшти гов	[gœʃti gov]
sausage (bologna, pepperoni, etc.)	ҳасиб	[hasib]

egg	тухм	[tuχm]
fish	моҳӣ	[mohi:]
cheese	панир	[panir]
sugar	шакар	[ʃakar]
salt	намак	[namak]

rice	биринҷ	[birindʒ]
pasta (macaroni)	макарон	[makaron]
butter	равғани маска	[ravʁani maska]
vegetable oil	равғани пок	[ravʁani pok]
bread	нон	[non]
chocolate (n)	шоколад	[ʃokolad]
wine	шароб, май	[ʃarob], [maj]
coffee	қаҳва	[qahva]
milk	шир	[ʃir]
juice	шарбат	[ʃarbat]
beer	пиво	[pivo]
tea	чой	[tʃoj]

tomato	помидор	[pomidor]
cucumber	бодиринг	[bodiriŋ]
carrot	сабзӣ	[sabzi:]
potato	картошка	[kartoʃka]
onion	пиёз	[pijɔz]
garlic	сир	[sir]
cabbage	карам	[karam]
beetroot	лаблабу	[lablabu]
eggplant	бодинҷон	[bodindʒon]
dill	шибит	[ʃibit]
lettuce	коҳу	[kohu]
corn (maize)	ҷуворимакка	[dʒuvorimakka]

fruit	мева	[meva]
apple	себ	[seb]
pear	мурӯд, нок	[murœd], [nok]
lemon	лиму	[limu]
orange	афлесун, пӯртахол	[aflesun], [pœrtaχol]
strawberry (garden ~)	қулфинай	[qulfinaj]

plum	олу	[olu]
raspberry	тамашк	[tamaʃk]
pineapple	ананас	[ananas]
banana	банан	[banan]
watermelon	тарбуз	[tarbuz]
grape	ангур	[angur]

12. Food. Part 2

| cuisine | таомҳо | [taomho] |
| recipe | ретсепт | [retsept] |

food	хӯрок, таом	[xœrok], [taom]
to have breakfast	ношита кардан	[noniʃta kardan]
to have lunch	хӯроки пешин хӯрдан	[xœroki peʃin xœrdan]
to have dinner	хӯроки шом хӯрдан	[xœroki ʃom xœrdan]

taste, flavor	маза, таъм	[maza], [ta'm]
tasty (adj)	бомаза	[bomaza]
cold (adj)	хунук	[xunuk]
hot (adj)	гарм	[garm]
sweet (sugary)	ширин	[ʃirin]
salty (adj)	шӯр	[ʃœr]

sandwich (bread)	бутерброд	[buterbrod]
side dish	хӯриши таом	[xœriʃi taom]
filling (for cake, pie)	пур кардани, андохтани	[pur kardani], [andoxtani]
sauce	қайла	[qajla]
piece (of cake, pie)	порча	[portʃa]

diet	диета	[dieta]
vitamin	витамин	[vitamin]
calorie	калория	[kalorija]
vegetarian (n)	гӯштнахӯранда	[gœʃtnaxœranda]

restaurant	тарабхона	[tarabxona]
coffee house	қаҳвахона	[qahvaxona]
appetite	иштиҳо	[iʃtiho]
Enjoy your meal!	ош шавад!	[oʃ ʃavad]

waiter	пешхизмат	[peʃxizmat]
waitress	пешхизмат	[peʃxizmat]
bartender	бармен	[barmen]
menu	меню	[menju]

spoon	қошуқ	[qoʃuq]
knife	корд	[kord]
fork	чангча, чангол	[tʃangtʃa], [tʃangol]
cup (e.g., coffee ~)	косача	[kosatʃa]

plate (dinner ~)	тақсимча	[taqsimtʃa]
saucer	тақсимй, тақсимича	[taqsimi:], [taqsimitʃa]
napkin (on table)	салфетка	[salfetka]
toothpick	дандонковак	[dandonkovak]

to order (meal)	супориш додан	[suporiʃ dodan]
course, dish	таом	[taom]
portion	навола	[navola]
appetizer	хӯриш, газак	[xœriʃ], [gazak]
salad	салат	[salat]
soup	шӯрбо	[ʃœrbo]

| dessert | десерт | [desert] |
| jam (whole fruit jam) | мураббо | [murabbo] |

ice-cream	яхмос	[jaχmos]
check	ҳисоб	[hisob]
to pay the check	пардохт кардан	[pardoχt kardan]
tip	чойпулй	[ʧojpuli:]

13. House. Apartment. Part 1

house	хона	[χona]
country house	хонаи берун аз шаҳр	[χonai berun az ʃahr]
villa (seaside ~)	кӯшк, чорбоғ	[kœʃk], [ʧorboʁ]

floor, story	қабат, ошёна	[qabat], [oʃjona]
entrance	даромадгоҳ	[daromadgoh]
wall	девор	[devor]
roof	бом	[bom]
chimney	мӯрии дудкаш	[mœri:i dudkaʃ]
attic (storage place)	чердак	[ʧerdak]
window	тиреза	[tireza]
window ledge	зертахтаи тиреза	[zertaχtai tireza]
balcony	балкон	[balkon]

stairs (stairway)	зина, зинапоя	[zina], [zinapoja]
mailbox	қуттии почта	[qutti:i poʧta]
garbage can	қуттии партов	[qutti:i partov]
elevator	лифт	[lift]

electricity	барқ	[barq]
light bulb	лампача, чароғча	[lampaʧa], [ʧaroʁʧa]
switch	калидак	[kalidak]
wall socket	розетка	[rozetka]
fuse	пешгирикунанда	[peʃgirikunanda]

door	дар	[dar]
handle, doorknob	дастак	[dastak]
key	калид	[kalid]
doormat	пойандоз	[pojandoz]

door lock	қулф	[qulf]
doorbell	занг	[zang]
knock (at the door)	тақ-тақ	[taq-taq]
to knock (vi)	тақ-тақ кардан	[taq-taq kardan]
peephole	чашмаки дар	[ʧaʃmaki dar]

yard	ҳавлӣ	[havli:]
garden	боғ	[boʁ]
swimming pool	ҳавз	[havz]
gym (home gym)	толори варзишӣ	[tolori varziʃi:]
tennis court	майдони теннис	[majdoni tennis]
garage	гараж	[garaʒ]
private property	мулки хусусӣ	[mulki χususi:]

warning sign	хати огоҳӣ	[χati ogohi:]
security	посбонӣ	[posboni:]
security guard	посбон	[posbon]

renovations	таъмир, тармим	[ta'mir], [tarmim]
to renovate (vt)	таъмир кардан	[ta'mir kardan]
to put in order	ба тартиб андохтан	[ba tartib andoχtan]
to paint (~ a wall)	ранг кардан	[rang kardan]
wallpaper	зардеворӣ	[zardevori:]
to varnish (vt)	лок задан	[lok zadan]

pipe	қубур	[qubur]
tools	асбобу анчом	[asbobu anʤom]
basement	таҳхона	[tahχona]
sewerage (system)	канализатсия	[kanalizatsija]

14. House. Apartment. Part 2

apartment	манзил	[manzil]
room	хона, ӯтоқ	[χona], [œtoq]
bedroom	хонаи хоб	[χonai χob]
dining room	хонаи хӯрокхӯрӣ	[χonai χœrokχœri:]

living room	меҳмонхона	[mehmonχona]
study (home office)	утоқ	[utoq]
entry room	мадхал, даҳлез	[madχal], [dahlez]
bathroom (room with a bath or shower)	ваннахона	[vannaχona]
half bath	ҳоҷатхона	[hoʤatχona]

| floor | фарш | [farʃ] |
| ceiling | шифт | [ʃift] |

to dust (vt)	чанг гирифтан	[ʧang giriftan]
vacuum cleaner	чангкашак	[ʧangkaʃak]
to vacuum (vt)	чанг кашидан	[ʧang kaʃidan]

mop	пайкора	[pajkora]
dust cloth	латта	[latta]
short broom	ҷорӯб	[ʤorœb]
dustpan	хокандози ахлот	[χokandozi aχlot]

furniture	мебел	[mebel]
table	миз	[miz]
chair	курсӣ	[kursi:]
armchair	курсӣ	[kursi:]

bookcase	чевони китобмонӣ	[ʤevoni kitobmoni:]
shelf	раф, рафча	[raf], [rafʧa]
wardrobe	чевони либос	[ʤevoni libos]

mirror	оина	[oina]
carpet	гилем, қолин	[gilem], [qolin]
fireplace	оташдон	[otaʃdon]
drapes	парда	[parda]
table lamp	чароғи мизӣ	[tʃaroʁi mizi:]
chandelier	қандил	[qandil]

kitchen	ошхона	[oʃxona]
gas stove (range)	плитаи газ	[plitai gaz]
electric stove	плитаи электрикӣ	[plitai ɛlektriki:]
microwave oven	микроволновка	[mikrovolnovka]

refrigerator	яхдон	[jaxdon]
freezer	яхдон	[jaxdon]
dishwasher	мошини зарфшӯй	[moʃini zarfʃœj]
faucet	чуммак, мил	[dʒummak], [mil]

meat grinder	мошини гӯштқӯбӣ	[moʃini gœʃtkœbi:]
juicer	шарбатафшурак	[ʃarbatafʃurak]
toaster	тостер	[toster]
mixer	миксер	[mikser]

coffee machine	қаҳвачӯшонак	[qahvadʒœʃonak]
kettle	чойник	[tʃojnik]
teapot	чойник	[tʃojnik]

TV set	телевизор	[televizor]
VCR (video recorder)	видеомагнитафон	[videomagnitafon]
iron (e.g., steam ~)	дарзмол	[darzmol]
telephone	телефон	[telefon]

15. Professions. Social status

director	директор, мудир	[direktor], [mudir]
superior	сардор	[sardor]
president	президент	[prezident]
assistant	ёвар	[jɔvar]
secretary	котиб	[kotib]

owner, proprietor	соҳиб	[sohib]
partner	шарик	[ʃarik]
stockholder	саҳмиядор	[sahmijador]

businessman	корчаллон	[kortʃallon]
millionaire	миллионер	[millioner]
billionaire	миллиардер	[milliarder]

actor	ҳунарманд	[hunarmand]
architect	меъмор	[me'mor]
banker	соҳиби банк	[sohiʁi bank]

broker	брокер	[broker]
veterinarian	духтури ҳайвонот	[duχturi hajvonot]
doctor	духтур	[duχtur]
chambermaid	пешхизмат	[peʃχizmat]
designer	дизайнгар, зебосоз	[dizajngar], [zebosoz]
correspondent	мухбир	[muχbir]
delivery man	хаткашон	[χatkaʃon]

electrician	барқчӣ	[barqtʃi:]
musician	мусиқачӣ	[musiqatʃi:]
babysitter	бачабардор	[batʃabardor]
hairdresser	сартарош	[sartaroʃ]
herder, shepherd	подабон	[podabon]

singer (masc.)	сурудхон, ҳофиз	[surudχon], [hofiz]
translator	тарҷумон	[tardʒumon]
writer	нависанда	[navisanda]
carpenter	дуредгар	[duredgar]
cook	ошпаз	[oʃpaz]

fireman	сӯхторхомӯшкун	[sœχtorχomœʃkun]
police officer	полис	[polis]
mailman	хаткашон	[χatkaʃon]
programmer	барномасоз	[barnomasoz]
salesman (store staff)	фурӯш	[furœʃ]

worker	коргар	[korgar]
gardener	боғбон	[boʁbon]
plumber	сантехник	[santeχnik]
dentist	дандонпизишк	[dandonpiziʃk]
flight attendant (fem.)	стюардесса	[stjuardessa]

dancer (masc.)	раққос	[raqqos]
bodyguard	муҳофиз	[muhofiz]
scientist	олим	[olim]
schoolteacher	муаллим	[muallim]

farmer	фермер	[fermer]
surgeon	ҷарроҳ	[dʒarroh]
miner	конкан	[konkan]
chef (kitchen chef)	сарошпаз	[saroʃpaz]
driver	рононда	[rononda]

16. Sport

kind of sports	намуди варзиш	[namudi varziʃ]
soccer	футбол	[futbol]
hockey	хоккей	[χokkej]
basketball	баскетбол	[basketbol]
baseball	бейсбол	[bejsbol]

volleyball	волейбол	[volejbol]
boxing	бокс	[boks]
wrestling	гӯштин	[gœʃtin]
tennis	теннис	[tennis]
swimming	шиноварӣ	[ʃinovari:]

chess	шоҳмот	[ʃohmot]
running	давидани	[davidani]
athletics	атлетикаи сабук	[atletikai sabuk]
figure skating	рақси рӯи ях	[raqsi rœi jaχ]
cycling	спорти велосипедронӣ	[sporti velosipedroni:]

billiards	билярдбозӣ	[biljardbozi:]
bodybuilding	бодибилдинг	[bodibilding]
golf	голф	[golf]
scuba diving	дайвинг	[dajving]
sailing	варзиши парусӣ	[varziʃi parusi:]
archery	камонварӣ	[kamonvari:]

period, half	тайм	[tajm]
half-time	танаффус	[tanaffus]
tie	дуранг	[durang]
to tie (vi)	бозиро дуранг кардан	[boziro durang kardan]

treadmill	роҳи пойга	[rohi pojga]
player	бозингар	[bozingar]
substitute	бозигари эҳтиётӣ	[bozigari ɛhtijoti:]
substitutes bench	нишастгоҳи бозингарони эҳтиётӣ	[niʃastgohi bozingaroni ɛhtijoti:]

match	вохӯрӣ	[voχœri:]
goal	дарвоза	[darvoza]
goalkeeper	дарвозабон	[darvozabon]
goal (score)	гол, хол	[gol], [χol]

Olympic Games	Бозиҳои олимпӣ	[bozihoi olimpi:]
to set a record	рекорд нишон додан	[rekord niʃon dodan]
final	финал	[final]
champion	чемпион	[tʃempion]
championship	чемпионат	[tʃempionat]

winner	ғолиб	[ʁolib]
victory	ғалаба	[ʁalaba]
to win (vi)	бурдан	[burdan]
to lose (not win)	бохтан	[boχtan]
medal	медал	[medal]

first place	ҷойи аввал	[dʒoji avval]
second place	ҷойи дуюм	[dʒoji dujum]
third place	ҷойи сеюм	[dʒoji sejum]
stadium	варзишгоҳ	[varziʃgoh]
fan, supporter	мухлис	[muχlis]

trainer, coach	тренер	[trener]
training	машқ	[maʃq]

17. Foreign languages. Orthography

language	забон	[zabon]
to study (vt)	омӯхтан	[omœχtan]
pronunciation	талаффуз	[talaffuz]
accent	зада, аксент	[zada], [aksent]
noun	исм	[ism]
adjective	сифат	[sifat]
verb	феъл	[fe'l]
adverb	зарф	[zarf]
pronoun	ҷонишин	[dʒoniʃin]
interjection	нидо	[nido]
preposition	пешоянд	[peʃojand]
root	решаи калима	[reʃai kalima]
ending	бандак	[bandak]
prefix	префикс	[prefiks]
syllable	ҳиҷо	[hidʒo]
suffix	суффикс	[suffiks]
stress mark	зада	[zada]
period, dot	нуқта	[nuqta]
comma	вергул	[vergul]
colon	ду нуқта	[du nuqta]
ellipsis	бисёрнуқта	[bisjornuqta]
question	савол	[savol]
question mark	аломати савол	[alomati savol]
exclamation point	аломати хитоб	[alomati χitob]
in quotation marks	дар нохунак	[dar noχunak]
in parenthesis	дар қавс	[dar qavs]
letter	ҳарф	[harf]
capital letter	ҳарфи калон	[harfi kalon]
sentence	ҷумла	[dʒumla]
group of words	ибора	[ibora]
expression	ибора	[ibora]
subject	мубтадо	[mubtado]
predicate	хабар	[χabar]
line	сатр, хат	[satr], [χat]
paragraph	сарсатр	[sarsatr]
synonym	муродиф	[murodif]
antonym	антоним	[antonim]

| exception | истисно | [istisno] |
| to underline (vt) | хат кашидан | [xat kaʃidan] |

rules	қоидаҳо	[qoidaho]
grammar	грамматика	[grammatika]
vocabulary	лексика	[leksika]
phonetics	савтиёт	[savtijɔt]
alphabet	алифбо	[alifbo]

textbook	китоби дарсӣ	[kitobi darsi:]
dictionary	луғат	[luʁat]
phrasebook	сӯҳбатнома	[sœhbatnoma]

word	калима	[kalima]
meaning	маънӣ, маъно	[ma'ni:], [ma'no]
memory	ҳофиза	[hofiza]

18. The Earth. Geography

the Earth	Замин	[zamin]
the globe (the Earth)	кураи замин	[kurai zamin]
planet	сайёра	[sajjɔra]

geography	география	[geografija]
nature	табиат	[tabiat]
map	харита	[xarita]
atlas	атлас	[atlas]

in the north	дар шимол	[dar ʃimol]
in the south	дар ҷануб	[dar dʒanub]
in the west	дар ғарб	[dar ʁarb]
in the east	дар шарқ	[dar ʃarq]

sea	баҳр	[bahr]
ocean	уқёнус	[uqjɔnus]
gulf (bay)	халиҷ	[xalidʒ]
straits	гулӯгоҳ	[gulœgoh]

continent (mainland)	материк, қитъа	[materik], [qit'a]
island	ҷазира	[dʒazira]
peninsula	нимҷазира	[nimdʒazira]
archipelago	галаҷазира	[galadʒazira]

harbor	бандар	[bandar]
coral reef	обсанги марҷонӣ	[obsangi mardʒoni:]
shore	соҳил, соҳили баҳр	[sohil], [sohili bahr]
coast	соҳил	[sohil]

| flow (flood tide) | мадд | [madd] |
| ebb (ebb tide) | ҷазр | [dʒazr] |

latitude	арз	[arz]
longitude	тӯл	[tœl]
parallel	параллел	[parallel]
equator	хати истиво	[χati istivo]

sky	осмон	[osmon]
horizon	уфуқ	[ufuq]
atmosphere	атмосфера	[atmosfera]

mountain	кӯҳ	[kœh]
summit, top	кулла	[kulla]
cliff	шух	[ʃuχ]
hill	теппа	[teppa]

volcano	вулқон	[vulqon]
glacier	пирях	[pirjaχ]
waterfall	шаршара	[ʃarʃara]
plain	ҳамворӣ	[hamvori:]

river	дарё	[darjɔ]
spring (natural source)	чашма	[tʃaʃma]
bank (of river)	соҳил	[sohil]
downstream (adv)	мувофиқи рафти об	[muvofiqi rafti ob]
upstream (adv)	муқобили самти об	[muqobili samti ob]

lake	кул	[kul]
dam	сарбанд	[sarband]
canal	канал	[kanal]
swamp (marshland)	ботлоқ, ботқоқ	[botloq], [botqoq]
ice	ях	[jaχ]

19. Countries of the world. Part 1

European Union	Иттиҳоди Аврупо	[ittihodi avrupo]
Austria	Австрия	[avstrija]
Great Britain	Инглистон	[ingliston]
England	Англия	[anglija]
Belgium	Белгия	[belgija]
Germany	Олмон	[olmon]

Netherlands	Ҳоланд	[holand]
Holland	Ҳолландия	[hollandija]
Greece	Юнон	[junon]
Denmark	Дания	[danija]
Ireland	Ирландия	[irlandija]

Iceland	Исландия	[islandija]
Spain	Испониё	[isponijɔ]
Italy	Итолиё	[itolijɔ]
Cyprus	Кипр	[kipr]

Malta	Малта	[malta]
Norway	Норвегия	[norvegija]
Portugal	Португалия	[portugalija]
Finland	Финланд	[finland]
France	Фаронса	[faronsa]
Sweden	Шветсия	[ʃvetsija]
Switzerland	Швейсария	[ʃvejsarija]
Scotland	Шотландия	[ʃotlandija]
Vatican	Вотикон	[votikon]
Liechtenstein	Лихтенштейн	[liҳtenʃtejn]
Luxembourg	Люксембург	[ljuksemburg]
Monaco	Монако	[monako]
Albania	Албания	[albanija]
Bulgaria	Булгористон	[bulʁoriston]
Hungary	Маҷористон	[maʤoriston]
Latvia	Латвия	[latvija]
Lithuania	Литва	[litva]
Poland	Полша, Лаҳистон	[polʃa], [lahiston]
Romania	Руминия	[ruminija]
Serbia	Сербия	[serbija]
Slovakia	Словакия	[slovakija]
Croatia	Хорватия	[ҳorvatija]
Czech Republic	Чехия	[ʧeҳija]
Estonia	Эстония	[ɛstonija]
Bosnia and Herzegovina	Босния ва Ҳерсеговина	[bosnija va hersegovina]
Macedonia (Republic of ~)	Мақдуния	[maqdunija]
Slovenia	Словения	[slovenija]
Montenegro	Монтенегро	[montenegro]
Belarus	Беларус	[belarus]
Moldova, Moldavia	Молдова	[moldova]
Russia	Россия	[rossija]
Ukraine	Украйина	[ukrajina]

20. Countries of the world. Part 2

Asia	Осиё	[osijo]
Vietnam	Ветнам	[vetnam]
India	Ҳиндустон	[hinduston]
Israel	Исроил	[isroil]
China	Чин	[ʧin]
Lebanon	Лубнон	[lubnon]
Mongolia	Муғулистон	[muʁuliston]
Malaysia	Малайзия	[malajzija]
Pakistan	Покистон	[pokiston]

Saudi Arabia	Арабистони Саудй	[arabistoni saudi:]
Thailand	Таиланд	[tailand]
Taiwan	Тайван	[tajvan]
Turkey	Туркия	[turkija]
Japan	Жопун, Чопон	[ʒopun], [dʒopon]
Afghanistan	Афғонистон	[afʁoniston]
Bangladesh	Бангладеш	[bangladeʃ]
Indonesia	Индонезия	[indonezija]
Jordan	Урдун	[urdun]
Iraq	Ироқ	[iroq]
Iran	Эрон	[ɛron]
Cambodia	Камбоча	[kambodʒa]
Kuwait	Кувайт	[kuvajt]
Laos	Лаос	[laos]
Myanmar	Мянма	[mjanma]
Nepal	Непал	[nepal]
United Arab Emirates	Иморатҳои Муттаҳидаи Араб	[imorathoi muttahidai arab]
Syria	Сурия	[surija]
Palestine	Фаластин	[falastin]
South Korea	Кореяи Ҷанубй	[korejai dʒanubi:]
North Korea	Кореяи Шимолй	[korejai ʃimoli:]
United States of America	Иёлоти Муттаҳидаи Америка	[ijɔloti muttahidai amerika]
Canada	Канада	[kanada]
Mexico	Мексика	[meksika]
Argentina	Аргентина	[argentina]
Brazil	Бразилия	[brazilija]
Colombia	Колумбия	[kolumbija]
Cuba	Куба	[kuba]
Chile	Чиле	[tʃile]
Venezuela	Венесуэла	[venesuɛla]
Ecuador	Эквадор	[ɛkvador]
The Bahamas	Ҷазираҳои Багам	[dʒazirahoi bagam]
Panama	Панама	[panama]
Egypt	Миср	[misr]
Morocco	Марокаш	[marokaʃ]
Tunisia	Тунис	[tunis]
Kenya	Кения	[kenija]
Libya	Либия	[libija]
South Africa	Африқои Ҷанубй	[afriqoi dʒanubi:]
Australia	Австралия	[avstralija]
New Zealand	Зеландияи Нав	[zelandijai nav]

21. Weather. Natural disasters

weather	обу ҳаво	[obu havo]
weather forecast	пешгӯии ҳаво	[peʃɡœi:i havo]
temperature	ҳарорат	[harorat]
thermometer	ҳароратсанҷ	[haroratsandʒ]
barometer	барометр, ҳавосанҷ	[barometr], [havosandʒ]
sun	офтоб	[oftob]
to shine (vi)	тобидан	[tobidan]
sunny (day)	… и офтоб	[i oftob]
to come up (vi)	баромадан	[baromadan]
to set (vi)	паст шудан	[past ʃudan]
rain	борон	[boron]
it's raining	борон меборад	[boron meborad]
pouring rain	борони сахт	[boroni saχt]
rain cloud	абри сиёҳ	[abri sijɔh]
puddle	кӯлмак	[kœlmak]
to get wet (in rain)	шилтиқ шудан	[ʃiltiq ʃudan]
thunderstorm	раъду барк	[ra'du bark]
lightning (~ strike)	барқ	[barq]
to flash (vi)	дурахшидан	[duraχʃidan]
thunder	тундар	[tundar]
it's thundering	раъд гулдуррос мезанад	[ra'd guldurros mezanad]
hail	жола	[ʒola]
it's hailing	жола меборад	[ʒola meborad]
heat (extreme ~)	гармӣ	[garmi:]
it's hot	ҳаво тафсон аст	[havo tafson ast]
it's warm	ҳаво гарм аст	[havo garm ast]
it's cold	ҳаво сард аст	[havo sard ast]
fog (mist)	туман	[tuman]
foggy	… и туман	[i tuman]
cloud	абр	[abr]
cloudy (adj)	… и абр, абрӣ	[i abr], [abri:]
humidity	намӣ, рутубат	[nami:], [rutubat]
snow	барф	[barf]
it's snowing	барф меборад	[barf meborad]
frost (severe ~, freezing cold)	хунукӣ	[χunuki:]
below zero (adv)	аз сифр поён	[az sifr pojɔn]
hoarfrost	қиров	[qirav]
bad weather	ҳавои бад	[havoi bad]
disaster	садама, фалокат	[sadama], [falokat]
flood, inundation	обхезӣ	[obχezi:]

| avalanche | тарма | [tarma] |
| earthquake | заминчунбӣ | [zamindʒunbi:] |

tremor, quake	заминчунбӣ,такон	[zamindʒunbi:,takon]
epicenter	эпимарказ	[ɛpimarkaz]
eruption	оташфишонӣ	[otaʃfiʃoni:]
lava	гудоза	[gudoza]

tornado	торнадо	[tornado]
twister	гирдбод	[girdbod]
hurricane	тундбод	[tundbod]
tsunami	сунами	[sunami]
cyclone	сиклон	[siklon]

22. Animals. Part 1

| animal | ҳайвон | [hajvon] |
| predator | дарранда | [darranda] |

tiger	бабр, паланг	[babr], [palang]
lion	шер	[ʃer]
wolf	гург	[gurg]
fox	рӯбоҳ	[rœboh]
jaguar	юзи ало	[juzi alo]

lynx	силовсин	[silovsin]
coyote	койот	[kojɔt]
jackal	шагол	[ʃagol]
hyena	кафтор	[kaftor]

squirrel	санҷоб	[sandʒob]
hedgehog	хорпушт	[χorpuʃt]
rabbit	харгӯш	[χargœʃ]
raccoon	енот	[enot]

hamster	миримӯшон	[mirimœʃon]
mole	кӯрмуш	[kœrmuʃ]
mouse	муш	[muʃ]
rat	калламуш	[kallamuʃ]
bat	кӯршапарак	[kœrʃaparak]

beaver	кундуз	[kunduz]
horse	асп	[asp]
deer	гавазн	[gavazn]
camel	шутур, уштур	[ʃutur], [uʃtur]
zebra	гӯрхар	[gœrχar]

whale	кит, наҳанг	[kit], [nahang]
seal	тюлен	[tjulen]
walrus	морж	[morʒ]

dolphin	делфин	[delfin]
bear	хирс	[xirs]
monkey	маймун	[majmun]
elephant	фил	[fil]
rhinoceros	карк, каркадан	[kark], [karkadan]
giraffe	заррофа	[zarrofa]

hippopotamus	баҳмут	[bahmut]
kangaroo	кенгуру	[kenguru]
cat	гурба	[gurba]
dog	саг	[sag]

cow	гов	[gov]
bull	барзагов	[barzagov]
sheep (ewe)	меш, гӯсфанд	[meʃ], [gœsfand]
goat	буз	[buz]

donkey	хар, маркаб	[xar], [markab]
pig, hog	хук	[xuq]
hen (chicken)	мург	[murʁ]
rooster	хурӯс	[xurœs]

duck	мургобй	[murʁobi:]
goose	қоз, ғоз	[qoz], [ʁoz]
turkey (hen)	мокиёни мурги марчон	[mokijoni murʁi mardʒon]
sheepdog	саги чӯпонй	[sagi ʧœponi:]

23. Animals. Part 2

bird	паранда	[paranda]
pigeon	кафтар	[kaftar]
sparrow	гунчишк, чумчук	[gundʒiʃk], [ʧumʧuk]
tit (great tit)	фотимачумчук	[fotimaʧumʧuq]
magpie	акка	[akka]

eagle	укоб	[ukob]
hawk	пайғу	[pajʁu]
falcon	боз, шоҳин	[boz], [ʃohin]

swan	қу	[qu]
crane	куланг, турна	[kulang], [turna]
stork	лаклак	[laklak]
parrot	тӯтй	[tœti:]
peacock	товус	[tovus]
ostrich	шутурмурғ	[ʃuturmurʁ]

heron	ҳавосил	[havosil]
nightingale	булбул	[bulbul]
swallow	фароштурук	[faroʃturuk]
cuckoo	фохтак	[foxtak]

owl	бум, чуғз	[bum], [dʒuʁz]
penguin	пингвин	[pingvin]
tuna	самак	[samak]
trout	гулмоҳй	[gulmohi:]
eel	мормоҳй	[mormohi:]

shark	наҳанг	[nahang]
crab	харчанг	[χartʃang]
jellyfish	медуза	[meduza]
octopus	ҳаштпо	[haʃtpo]

starfish	ситораи баҳрй	[sitorai bahri:]
sea urchin	хорпушти баҳрй	[χorpuʃti bahri:]
seahorse	аспакмоҳй	[aspakmohi:]
shrimp	креветка	[krevetka]

snake	мор	[mor]
viper	мори афъй	[mori afʔi:]
lizard	калтакалос	[kaltakalos]
iguana	сусмор, игуана	[susmor], [iguana]
chameleon	бӯқаламун	[bœqalamun]
scorpion	каждум	[kaʒdum]

turtle	сангпушт	[sangpuʃt]
frog	қурбоққа	[qurboqqa]
crocodile	тимсоҳ	[timsoh]

insect, bug	ҳашарот	[haʃarot]
butterfly	шапалак	[ʃapalak]
ant	мӯрча	[mœrtʃa]
fly	магас	[magas]

mosquito	пашша	[paʃʃa]
beetle	гамбуск	[gambusk]
bee	занбӯри асал	[zanbœri asal]
spider	тортанак	[tortanak]

24. Trees. Plants

tree	дарахт	[daraχt]
birch	тӯс	[tœs]
oak	булут	[bulut]
linden tree	зерфун	[zerfun]
aspen	сиёҳбед	[sijɔhbed]

maple	заранг	[zarang]
spruce	коч, ел	[kodʒ], [el]
pine	санавбар	[sanavbar]
cedar	дарахти чалғӯза	[daraχti dʒalʁœza]
poplar	сафедор	[safedor]

rowan	губайро	[ʁubajro]
beech	бук, олаш	[buk], [olaʃ]
elm	дарахти ларг	[daraχti larg]

ash (tree)	шумтол	[ʃumtol]
chestnut	шохбулут	[ʃohbulut]
palm tree	нахл	[naχl]
bush	бутта	[butta]

mushroom	занбӯруғ	[zanbœruʁ]
poisonous mushroom	занбӯруғи захрнок	[zanbœruʁi zahrnok]
cep (Boletus edulis)	занбӯруғи сафед	[zanbœruʁi safed]
russula	занбӯруғи хомхӯрак	[zanbœruʁi χomχœrak]
fly agaric	маргимагас	[margimagas]
death cap	занбӯруғи захрнок	[zanbœruʁi zahrnok]

flower	гул	[gul]
bouquet (of flowers)	дастаи гул	[dastai gul]
rose (flower)	гул, гули садбарг	[gul], [guli sadbarg]

| tulip | лола | [lola] |
| carnation | гули мехак | [guli meχak] |

camomile	бобуна	[bobuna]
cactus	гули ханчарӣ	[guli χandʒari:]
lily of the valley	гули барфак	[guli barfak]

| snowdrop | бойчечак | [bojtʃetʃak] |
| water lily | нилуфари сафед | [nilufari safed] |

greenhouse (tropical ~)	гулхона	[gulχona]
lawn	чаман, сабзазор	[tʃaman], [sabzazor]
flowerbed	гулзор	[gulzor]

plant	растанӣ	[rastani:]
grass	алаф	[alaf]
leaf	барг	[barg]
petal	гулбарг	[gulbarg]

| stem | поя | [poja] |
| young plant (shoot) | неш | [neʃ] |

| cereal crops | растанихои ғалладона | [rastanihoi ʁalladona] |
| wheat | гандум | [gandum] |

| rye | чавдор | [dʒavdor] |
| oats | хуртумон | [hurtumon] |

millet	арзан	[arzan]
barley	чав	[dʒav]
corn	чуворимакка	[dʒuvorimakka]
rice	шолӣ, биринч	[ʃoli:], [birindʒ]

25. Various useful words

balance (of situation)	мизон	[mizon]
base (basis)	асос	[asos]
beginning	сар	[sar]
category	категория	[kategorija]
choice	интихоб	[intiχob]
coincidence	рост омадани	[rost omadani]
comparison	муқоисакунӣ	[muqoisakuni:]
degree (extent, amount)	дараҷа	[daradʒa]
development	пешравӣ	[peʃravi:]
difference	фарқ, тафриқа	[farq], [tafriqa]
effect (e.g., of drugs)	таъсир	[ta'sir]
effort (exertion)	саъю кӯшиш	[sa'ju kœʃiʃ]
element	элемент	[ɛlement]
example (illustration)	мисол, назира	[misol], [nazira]
fact	факт	[fakt]
help	кумак	[kumak]
ideal	идеал	[ideal]
kind (sort, type)	навъ	[nav']
mistake, error	хато	[χato]
moment	лаҳза, дам	[lahza], [dam]
obstacle	монеа	[monea]
part (~ of sth)	қисм	[qism]
pause (break)	фосила	[fosila]
position	мавқеъ	[mavqe']
problem	масъала	[mas'ala]
process	ҷараён	[dʒarajon]
progress	тараққӣ	[taraqqi:]
property (quality)	хосият	[χosijat]
reaction	аксуламал	[aksulamal]
risk	хатар, таваккал	[χatar], [tavakkal]
secret	сир, роз	[sir], [roz]
series	силсила	[silsila]
shape (outer form)	шакл	[ʃakl]
situation	вазъият	[vaz'ijat]
solution	ҳал	[hal]
standard (adj)	стандартӣ	[standarti:]
stop (pause)	танаффус	[tanaffus]
style	услуб	[uslub]
system	тартиб	[tartib]

| table (chart) | чадвал | [dʒadval] |
| tempo, rate | суръат | [sur'at] |

term (word, expression)	истилоҳ	[istiloh]
truth (e.g., moment of ~)	ҳақиқат	[haqiqat]
turn (please wait your ~)	навбат	[navbat]
urgent (adj)	зуд, фаврӣ	[zud], [favri:]

utility (usefulness)	фоида	[foida]
variant (alternative)	вариант	[variant]
way (means, method)	тарз	[tarz]
zone	минтақа	[mintaqa]

26. Modifiers. Adjectives. Part 1

additional (adj)	иловагӣ	[ilovagi:]
ancient (~ civilization)	қадим	[qadim]
artificial (adj)	сунъӣ	[sun'i:]
bad (adj)	бад	[bad]
beautiful (person)	зебо	[zebo]

big (in size)	калон, бузург	[kalon], [buzurg]
bitter (taste)	талх	[talχ]
blind (sightless)	кӯр	[kœr]
central (adj)	марказӣ	[markazi:]

children's (adj)	бачагона, кӯдакона	[batʃagona], [kœdakona]
clandestine (secret)	пинҳонӣ	[pinhoni:]
clean (free from dirt)	тоза	[toza]
clever (smart)	оқил	[oqil]
compatible (adj)	мутобиқ	[mutobiq]

contented (satisfied)	хурсанд	[χursand]
dangerous (adj)	хатарнок	[χatarnok]
dead (not alive)	мурда	[murda]
dense (fog, smoke)	зич	[zitʃ]
difficult (decision)	душвор	[duʃvor]

dirty (not clean)	чиркин	[tʃirkin]
easy (not difficult)	осон	[oson]
empty (glass, room)	холӣ	[χoli:]
exact (amount)	аниқ	[aniq]
excellent (adj)	хуб	[χub]

excessive (adj)	аз ҳад зиёд	[az had zijod]
exterior (adj)	берунӣ, зоҳирӣ	[beruni:], [zohiri:]
fast (quick)	босуръат	[bosur'at]
fertile (land, soil)	серҳосил	[serhosil]
fragile (china, glass)	зудшикан	[zudʃikan]
free (at no cost)	бепул	[bepul]

fresh (~ water)	ширин	[ʃirin]
frozen (food)	яхкарда	[jaχkarda]
full (completely filled)	пур	[pur]
happy (adj)	хушбахт	[χuʃbaχt]
hard (not soft)	сахт	[saχt]
huge (adj)	бузург	[buzurg]
ill (sick, unwell)	касал, бемор	[kasal], [bemor]
immobile (adj)	беҳаракат	[beharakat]
important (adj)	муҳим, зарур	[muhim], [zarur]
interior (adj)	даруни	[daruni:]
last (e.g., ~ week)	гузашта	[guzaʃta]
last (final)	охирин	[oχirin]
left (e.g., ~ side)	чап	[ʧap]
legal (legitimate)	конуни, … и конун	[konuni:], [i konun]
light (in weight)	сабук	[sabuk]
liquid (fluid)	моеъ	[moe']
long (e.g., ~ hair)	дур	[dur]
loud (voice, etc.)	баланд	[baland]
low (voice)	паст	[past]

27. Modifiers. Adjectives. Part 2

main (principal)	асоси, муҳим	[asosi:], [muhim]
matt, matte	бечило	[beʤilo]
mysterious (adj)	асроромез	[asroromez]
narrow (street, etc.)	танг	[tang]
native (~ country)	… и ватан	[i vatan]
negative (~ response)	манфи	[manfi:]
new (adj)	нав	[nav]
next (e.g., ~ week)	оянда, навбати	[ojanda], [navbati:]
normal (adj)	мӯътадил	[mœ'tadil]
not difficult (adj)	сабук, осон	[sabuk], [oson]
obligatory (adj)	ҳатми	[hatmi:]
old (house)	кӯҳна	[kœhna]
open (adj)	кушод	[kuʃod]
opposite (adj)	муқобил	[muqobil]
ordinary (usual)	одди, одати	[oddi:], [odati:]
original (unusual)	бикр	[bikr]
personal (adj)	шахси	[ʃaχsi:]
polite (adj)	боадаб, боназокат	[boadab], [bonazokat]
poor (not rich)	камбағал	[kambaʁal]
possible (adj)	имконпазир	[imkonpazir]
principal (main)	асоси	[asosi:]

probable (adj)	эҳтимолӣ	[ɛhtimoli:]
prolonged (e.g., ~ applause)	давомнок	[davomnok]
public (open to all)	ҷамъиятӣ, оммавӣ	[dʒam'ijati:], [ommavi:]
rare (adj)	нодир	[nodir]
raw (uncooked)	хом	[χom]
right (not left)	рост	[rost]
ripe (fruit)	пухта	[puχta]
risky (adj)	хатарнок	[χatarnok]
sad (~ look)	ғамгин	[ʁamgin]
second hand (adj)	истифодабурдашуда	[istifodaburdaʃuda]
shallow (water)	камоб, пастоб	[kamob], [pastob]
sharp (blade, etc.)	тез	[tez]
short (in length)	кӯтоҳ	[kœtoh]
similar (adj)	монанд, шабеҳ	[monand], [ʃabeh]
small (in size)	хурд	[χurd]
smooth (surface)	ҳамвор	[hamvor]
soft (~ toys)	нарм, мулоим	[narm], [muloim]
solid (~ wall)	мустаҳкам	[mustahkam]
sour (flavor, taste)	турш	[turʃ]
spacious (house, etc.)	васеъ	[vase']
special (adj)	махсус	[maχsus]
straight (line, road)	рост	[rost]
strong (person)	зӯр, бақувват	[zœr], [baquvvat]
stupid (foolish)	аҳмак, аблаҳ	[ahmak], [ablah]
superb, perfect (adj)	олӣ	[oli:]
sweet (sugary)	ширин	[ʃirin]
tan (adj)	гандумгун	[gandumgun]
tasty (delicious)	бомаза	[bomaza]
unclear (adj)	норавшан	[noravʃan]

28. Verbs. Part 1

to accuse (vt)	айбдор кардан	[ajbdor kardan]
to agree (say yes)	розигӣ додан	[rozigi: dodan]
to announce (vt)	эълон кардан	[ɛ'lon kardan]
to answer (vi, vt)	ҷавоб додан	[dʒavob dodan]
to apologize (vi)	узр пурсидан	[uzr pursidan]
to arrive (vi)	расидан	[rasidan]
to ask (~ oneself)	пурсидан	[pursidan]
to be absent	набудан	[nabudan]
to be afraid	тарсидан	[tarsidan]
to be born	таваллуд шудан	[tavallud ʃudan]

to be in a hurry	шитоб кардан	[ʃitob kardan]
to beat (to hit)	задан	[zadan]
to begin (vt)	сар кардан	[sar kardan]
to believe (in God)	бовар доштан	[bovar doʃtan]
to belong to …	таалук доштан	[taaluq doʃtan]
to break (split into pieces)	шикастан	[ʃikastan]

to build (vt)	бино кардан	[bino kardan]
to buy (purchase)	харидан	[χaridan]
can (v aux)	тавонистан	[tavonistan]
can (v aux)	тавонистан	[tavonistan]
to cancel (call off)	бекор кардан	[bekor kardan]

to catch (vt)	доштан	[doʃtan]
to change (vt)	иваз кардан	[ivaz kardan]
to check (to examine)	тафтиш кардан	[taftiʃ kardan]
to choose (select)	интихоб кардан	[intiχob kardan]
to clean up (tidy)	рӯбучин кардан	[rœbutʃin kardan]

to close (vt)	пӯшидан, бастан	[pœʃidan], [bastan]
to compare (vt)	мукоиса кардан	[muqoisa kardan]
to complain (vi, vt)	шикоят кардан	[ʃikojat kardan]

| to confirm (vt) | тасдик кардан | [tasdiq kardan] |
| to congratulate (vt) | муборакбод гуфтан | [muborakbod guftan] |

to cook (dinner)	пухтан	[puχtan]
to copy (vt)	нусха бардоштан	[nusχa bardoʃtan]
to cost (vt)	арзидан	[arzidan]

| to count (add up) | ҳисоб кардан | [hisob kardan] |
| to count on … | умед бастан | [umed bastan] |

to create (vt)	офаридан	[ofaridan]
to cry (weep)	гиря кардан	[girja kardan]
to dance (vi, vt)	раксидан	[raqsidan]

| to deceive (vi, vt) | фирефтан | [fireftan] |
| to decide (~ to do sth) | карор додан | [qaror dodan] |

to delete (vt)	нобуд кардан	[nobud kardan]
to demand (request firmly)	талаб кардан	[talab kardan]
to deny (vt)	инкор кардан	[inkor kardan]

| to depend on … | мутеъ будан | [mute' budan] |
| to despise (vt) | ҳакорат кардан | [haqorat kardan] |

to die (vi)	мурдан	[murdan]
to dig (vt)	кофтан	[koftan]
to disappear (vi)	гум шудан	[gum ʃudan]
to discuss (vt)	мухокима кардан	[muhokima kardan]
to disturb (vt)	ташвиш додан	[taʃviʃ dodan]

29. Verbs. Part 2

to dive (vi)	ғӯта задан	[ʁœta zadan]
to divorce (vi)	талоқ гирифтан	[taloq giriftan]
to do (vt)	кардан	[kardan]
to doubt (have doubts)	шак доштан	[ʃak doʃtan]
to drink (vi, vt)	нӯшидан	[nœʃidan]
to drop (let fall)	афтондан	[aftondan]
to dry (clothes, hair)	хушк кардан	[χuʃk kardan]
to eat (vi, vt)	хӯрдан	[χœrdan]
to end (~ a relationship)	бас кардан	[bas kardan]
to excuse (forgive)	афв кардан	[afv kardan]
to exist (vi)	зиндагӣ кардан	[zindagi: kardan]
to expect (foresee)	пешбинӣ кардан	[peʃbini: kardan]
to explain (vt)	шарҳ додан	[ʃarh dodan]
to fall (vi)	афтодан	[aftodan]
to fight (street fight, etc.)	занозанӣ кардан	[zanozani: kardan]
to find (vt)	ёфтан	[jɔftan]
to finish (vt)	тамом кардан	[tamom kardan]
to fly (vi)	паридан	[paridan]
to forbid (vt)	манъ кардан	[man' kardan]
to forget (vi, vt)	фаромӯш кардан	[faromœʃ kardan]
to forgive (vt)	бахшидан	[baχʃidan]
to get tired	монда шудан	[monda ʃudan]
to give (vt)	додан	[dodan]
to go (on foot)	рафтан	[raftan]
to hate (vt)	нафрат кардан	[nafrat kardan]
to have (vt)	доштан	[doʃtan]
to have breakfast	ноништа кардан	[noniʃta kardan]
to have dinner	хӯроки шом хӯрдан	[χœroki ʃom χœrdan]
to have lunch	хӯроки пешин хӯрдан	[χœroki peʃin χœrdan]
to hear (vt)	шунидан	[ʃunidan]
to help (vt)	кумак кардан	[kumak kardan]
to hide (vt)	пинҳон кардан	[pinhon kardan]
to hope (vi, vt)	умед доштан	[umed doʃtan]
to hunt (vi, vt)	шикор кардан	[ʃikor kardan]
to hurry (vi)	шитоб кардан	[ʃitob kardan]
to insist (vi, vt)	сахт истодан	[saχt istodan]
to insult (vt)	таҳқир кардан	[tahqir kardan]
to invite (vt)	даъват кардан	[da'vat kardan]
to joke (vi)	шӯхӣ кардан	[ʃœχi: kardan]
to keep (vt)	нигоҳ доштан	[nigoh doʃtan]
to kill (vt)	куштан	[kuʃtan]
to know (sb)	донистан	[donistan]

to know (sth)	донистан	[donistan]
to like (I like …)	форидан	[foridan]
to look at …	нигоҳ кардан ба …	[nigoh kardan ba]
to lose (umbrella, etc.)	гум кардан	[gum kardan]
to love (sb)	дӯст доштан	[dœst doʃtan]
to make a mistake	хато кардан	[χato kardan]
to meet (vi, vt)	мулоқот кардан	[muloqot kardan]
to miss (school, etc.)	набудан	[nabudan]

30. Verbs. Part 3

to obey (vi, vt)	зердаст шудан	[zerdast ʃudan]
to open (vt)	кушодан	[kuʃodan]
to participate (vi)	иштирок кардан	[iʃtirok kardan]
to pay (vi, vt)	пул додан	[pul dodan]
to permit (vt)	иҷозат додан	[idʒozat dodan]
to play (children)	бозӣ кардан	[bozi: kardan]
to pray (vi, vt)	намоз хондан	[namoz χondan]
to promise (vt)	ваъда додан	[va'da dodan]
to propose (vt)	таклиф кардан	[taklif kardan]
to prove (vt)	исбот кардан	[isbot kardan]
to read (vi, vt)	хондан	[χondan]
to receive (vt)	гирифтан	[giriftan]
to rent (sth from sb)	ба иҷора гирифтан	[ba idʒora giriftan]
to repeat (say again)	такрор кардан	[takror kardan]
to reserve, to book	нигоҳ доштан	[nigoh doʃtan]
to run (vi)	давидан	[davidan]
to save (rescue)	наҷот додан	[nadʒot dodan]
to say (~ thank you)	гуфтан	[guftan]
to see (vt)	дидан	[didan]
to sell (vt)	фурӯхтан	[furœχtan]
to send (vt)	ирсол кардан	[irsol kardan]
to shoot (vi)	тир задан	[tir zadan]
to shout (vi)	дод задан	[dod zadan]
to show (vt)	нишон додан	[niʃon dodan]
to sign (document)	имзо кардан	[imzo kardan]
to sing (vi)	хондан	[χondan]
to sit down (vi)	нишастан	[niʃastan]
to smile (vi)	табассум кардан	[tabassum kardan]
to speak (vi, vt)	гап задан	[gap zadan]
to steal (money, etc.)	дуздидан	[duzdidan]
to stop (please ~ calling me)	бас кардан	[bas kardan]
to study (vt)	омӯхтан	[omœχtan]

to swim (vi)	шино кардан	[ʃino kardan]
to take (vt)	гирифтан	[giriftan]
to talk to …	гап задан бо …	[gap zadan bo]
to tell (story, joke)	нақл кардан	[naql kardan]
to thank (vt)	сипосгузорӣ кардан	[siposguzori: kardan]
to think (vi, vt)	фикр кардан	[fikr kardan]
to translate (vt)	тарҷума кардан	[tardʒuma kardan]
to trust (vt)	бовар кардан	[bovar kardan]
to try (attempt)	кӯшидан	[kœʃidan]
to turn (e.g., ~ left)	гардонидан	[gardonidan]
to turn off	куштан	[kuʃtan]
to turn on	даргирондан	[dargirondan]
to understand (vt)	фаҳмидан	[fahmidan]
to wait (vt)	поидан	[poidan]
to want (wish, desire)	хостан	[χostan]
to work (vi)	кор кардан	[kor kardan]
to write (vt)	навиштан	[naviʃtan]

www.ingramcontent.com/pod-product-compliance
Lightning Source LLC
Chambersburg PA
CBHW070115070426
42448CB00039B/2879